Breakup Cocktail

5 Parts Laughter, 1 Part Healing and a Twist of Revenge

BARBARA KINGSLEY SINGER

Copyright © 2012 Barbara Kingsley Singer
All rights reserved.

ISBN: 1480037850
ISBN-13: 9781480037854
Library of Congress Control Number: 2012918622
CreateSpace, North Charleston, South Carolina

Contents

PART TWO
THE RELATIONSHIP GHOST LINGERS ON
A Shot of Raw Emotions, Pity Sex and Ex-Talk

PART THREE
COMING TO TERMS WITH THE BREAKUP
A Spritzer of Memories, Coping and Thievery

PART FOUR
PICKING UP THE PIECES
A Snifter of Exorcism,
Responsibility and Time Travel

PART FIVE
HEALING
A Keg of Independence, Dating and Rebuilding

Introduction

A breakup is a sorry state of affairs and turning bad experiences and devastating events into funny stories is like making the best of Russian roulette. You might not think it can be done, but there's always someone who's willing to give it a try. Against all reason, I am that someone. Maybe I'm a masochist who has no shame or maybe I need to have a little more respect for a loaded gun. All of these tales are taken from my life experiences and are dressed up to look like they belong to someone else. Many are nourished with a shot of poetic license, but surprisingly, it's the most unbelievable events that are closest to the truth. When the ordinary is nowhere to be found, the extraordinary can be found in every home; under a dim street light; or sitting nonchalantly on a Greyhound bus. Strange events occur all around us and that's what makes a compelling story. In these short tales, humor softens the dilemmas, or if that fails, a cheap laugh is offered. These stories tell of small problems that grow out of proportion, just as it happens in real life, and the characters in them find themselves inept when dealing with their own predicaments. They over-emote, over-react and over-analyze. They are just too human. But their stories make entertaining reading that everyone can relate to and the valuable comments that follow each tale are cheerful and supportive, but not meant to be construed as expert advice!

Part One begins with tales of deception, confusion and revenge, or just plain boredom that occurs at the beginning of a breakup. These are the detonators that spark a life without your ex. What dirty little secret is your partner hiding from you? We might identify just a little too well with the tale of Donna, the suspicious spouse who spies on her partner, or perhaps we regrettably broke up our long-term relationship because of feelings of lust for someone new, just like in Marc's story.

A new life alone is depicted in Part Two—waking up in an unfamiliar home where you might have downgraded from grandeur to ghetto, and the shock makes you feel like you have just been smacked over the head with the breakup stick. Still missing your departed love, you might have kept a few of their unwanted belongings to treasure, and will therefore be able to relate to the dark, humorous pathos of Martin's story and his loving treatment of Kathy's discarded junk.

As we torture ourselves with memories of happier times with our ex, we forget that the mind often plays tricks on us, turning the bad times into good ones. Danny mistakenly recalls his life with Ella as being harmonious, especially when he cooked for her. He erroneously remembers the times when she glorified his goulash and honored his omelets, when in fact she mocked his macaroni and criticized his croutons. It's happened to the best of us and as the characters in Part Three struggle to come to terms with their new single lives, Lucy finds a way to overcome the holiday blues and

Andy cleverly devises a method to clone his girlfriends into replicas of his ex.

A cautionary tale of casual sex in Part Four will give you chills, as will the fable-like story of an ex-love who haunts their previous partner's home. And while we may smile at the story of DMV phobia, we may squirm at what Keith asks Alice to do in order to stay friends with him after their breakup.

In the final chapter, stories of online dating may impress, as we admire those who have tried and succeeded; whereas a tale of dating failure might be the stuff of which our nightmares are made. Whatever your reaction, you will be able to laugh it off because there's nothing better than knowing we are not alone in our troubled times and that others have suffered, just like us. You don't have to be sad to read these stories, but if you are, you won't be for long.

This collection of tales could be a companion to the lingering memory a piece of sweet chocolate leaves behind on the tongue, or the breath-catching warmth of a cocktail. Maybe it's a relaxing follow-up to your favorite TV show, but it will distract you from the loitering memories of your ex-lover, who is perhaps halfway to another state now or hopefully in the midst of a meaningless fight with their new partner.

So if it's a sunny day and you feel like having a drink, or even if it's a wintry day with the wind blowing icy all around your shoulders and you are in the mood for some cheer, take a little paper umbrella and put it inside the *Breakup Cocktail*. Just like any cocktail, it's a concoction of ingredients. This one begins with a smooth base of sweet talk and lies, followed by a twist of perverse revenge, a shot of rage, then thinned into a cloudy brew with tragedy as a mixer. A little sweetness of healing is added and the whole thing is stirred by a bitter shard of re-dating fear. After a while the liquid settles, you take a drink, and life is sweet again.

PART ONE

THE EXPIRING RELATIONSHIP

A Tall Glass of Revenge, Lust and Betrayal

Revenge for Cheating
Hair today, all washed out by tomorrow

*M*anipulation should really be considered a super-power. For instance, if we are guilty of exploiting our partners, there should be a Superhero who blazes their way into our homes and aims their anti-manipulation gun at our heads. We often can't help ourselves, but trying to change people or making them do something against their will is an evil gift we are born with, like scheming or taking the last cookie. It's a known fact we use our good qualities to benefit others, while our evil attributes are used to benefit only us—and look, there lays sin, hiding under the table! Cheating is one of those deeds born from our evil traits, and manipulation is its mealy-mouthed, bowlegged sidekick.

We can often sense when our partner is cheating, they may sneak around and lie to us. But if we feel manipulated by our mate and can't quite figure out why, we look for clues in seemingly normal behavior. In the tale below, Jan becomes suspicious when Quentin suggests changes in her look. Suspicion can bring on confusion and possibly a dinnertime hunger for revenge. If you believe you are being made to do things to enable your partner's cheating ways, you may turn to that deceptive person and say, "You'll be sorry!" But how sorry do you want to make them? Do you really want payback? Everyone feels anger when they are let down or deceived, and it is worse when someone makes a fool out of you. That's when a taste of vengeance calms the nerves, like a tranquilizer on the tongue.

The Tale of Jan

Quentin and Jan each had a sense of adventure that provided the gum in the relationship that kept them together. Quentin was a bright man who wore the deviousness gene tucked away where no one could see it, but on the outside he was a charmer with a zest for life. Jan's intelligence sparked less bright, although her hair was bright and brassy around the roots. She was a free spirit and owned a friendly smile she used generously most days. They had been married for nine years when Quentin came home one summer's day with an unusual gift for his wife.

Jan was hesitant in taking the brown paper sack he offered her, because good gifts usually come prettily wrapped and often with a bow. Groceries, wine and pornography came in plain wrappers and Jan felt she was not a plain girl. Quentin smiled as she dipped her hand gingerly into the bag without first looking inside. As her hand encountered what felt like human hair, she screamed, dropping the mystery bag onto the floor. "What is it?" she shrieked. "A shrunken head?" Quentin laughed as he retrieved the bag and removed the contents and she saw it was indeed human hair. It was a wig. A long, luxuriant auburn wig. Jan stared at it, transfixed, as Quentin modeled it on his hand for her, turning it this way and that, the way a fat pony shakes its mane as it struts around The Big Top.

"Do you like it?" he asked her enthusiastically. Jan wasn't sure. "I saw it in the window of the wig store on Ferry

Street and I thought it would match your beautiful gray eyes perfectly." He had her in flattery mode and she eased into the compliment without a backward glance.

"Really?"

"Oh yes. Here—take it," he handed it over to her. "It's very soft."

Jan prided herself on being adventurous, and she tried the red wig on right away. It felt a little warm around the forehead and tight around the ears and the weight of it was cumbersome, but then she saw the look on Quentin's face. She had read the phrase *unbridled lust* many times in her romance novels and it always conjured up a thrill, and now here was Quentin wearing the exact look just as she had pictured it. With rampant anticipation (another phrase from the romance novels) she ran to the hall mirror and saw a stranger. There was a sexy woman looking back at her. It was her, but she looked completely different and alluring. How cool was that? She noticed Quentin reflected in the mirror behind her. He had a glazed look in his eyes that she had never seen before and he appeared to be holding his breath.

When she wore the wig in bed that night it slid off and so eventually she had to take it off, but bed and the shower were the only times it wasn't on her head. Unfortunately her wardrobe wasn't suited to the color red, and when she wore a blue and yellow blouse along with the wig, Quentin remarked it made her resemble a flag from the European Union. Nevertheless, it made her feel free and gave her a sense of "anything can happen." She told Quentin that when she wore it, she felt like an actress and she built herself a whole seductive personality around it. Quentin loved to see her in the wig and he encouraged her to put it on.

One Thursday evening, right before Jan started making the evening meal, she went through Quentin's papers to look for the dry cleaning receipt. Rummaging through some papers on his dresser she came upon a small photograph of herself and Quentin laughing on the beach. She was wearing a black bikini and the long red wig. She stared at the photograph, taxing her mind for a spark of remembrance of that day. For a moment, an itchy feather of unreality tickled the back of her neck, just like the auburn wig did when she swung her head around quickly. She looked more closely at the woman. It wasn't her. But it was her hair on someone else, someone younger. Somebody who looked happy with her husband, and sadly for Jan, as she noticed the freckles, it seemed that the Someone Else had natural long, red hair.

Jan walked to her wig stand and stared at the wig and tried to make sense of what she had seen. Did Quentin like auburn hair so much that every girlfriend had to be a redhead? But why would he have a photograph of an old girlfriend on his dresser? She dusted the dresser once a week and would have seen it before if it was an old photo. It had to be a new one. Then another awful thought struck her. Had Quentin made her into a replica of a current girlfriend or a lost love? Did he like this other girl so much that he wanted Jan to look like her instead of looking like herself? If that were true, it would be the biggest insult of them all.

With the riddle going round and round in her head like a diagram of infinity, taking action was her next step. She went into the kitchen, took out a dinner plate from the cabinet and placed two slices of white bread on it. Then she took the butter from the refrigerator and buttered the bread. Next, she went back into the bedroom and removed the wig from the stand and brought it into the kitchen. She took the large scissors with the blue handles from the kitchen drawer and snipped off several long strands of the wig's red hair, and arranged them artistically onto the buttered bread.

Taking the photograph of her husband and Young Red, she cut out the face of Young Red and set it carefully in the middle of the buttered bread, where it looked up smilingly for only a second before it was hit in the eye with a few drops of hot pepper sauce. The happy, smiling face turned into a gruesome smiling one, as an image of hot pepper blood dripped down onto her cute little pixie chin. Her smiling green eyes held a glazed look as the second slice of buttered bread smeared across her face. Jan garnished the meal with a chef's practiced creativity, decorating it with a pickle and several slices of tomato sprinkled with dill, and the banquet was complete. Putting the plate on the table she called Quentin in for dinner, and for a little auburn confrontation.

Comment

Those who are scorned may take revenge to a whole new level when they strike back, but don't look to them as your role model. Luckily Jan's revenge was spread thin across the dinner of confrontation otherwise Quentin might have been facing a breakfast of burnt feud and jam alongside his coffee. While Jan used culinary punishment to ease the humiliation Quentin had caused her, other kinds of partner punishment exist, none of which should be encouraged. For example, there is the *withholding sex retaliation*; the *bad blood silent treatment*; and the ever-popular *mother-in-law vendetta*. But don't try any of these at home, where the best remedy is to have a peaceful confrontation to clear the air. If need be, a smattering of threats and a double shot of tears can go a long way, because now the tables are turned as you take over the role of manipulator.

But we'll never know if Jan gave Quentin a chance to defend himself, because after all, he may not have been cheating. So who was the mystery woman with him in the photograph and was she the inspiration for all of Quentin's lovers? It could be; or maybe she really was his current girlfriend.

Sometimes a cold shoulder and a chilled pat of butter can silently tell someone you are better off without them. Doing something really damaging out of jealousy can get you into physical trouble, or at least give you a sleepless night if your conscience disapproves of what you have done. If taken too far, the police might come knocking on your door. Once locked up behind bars you may become consumed with other jealousies, perhaps of Tattooed Tiffnee spending too much time with your bitch, Homicide Cindy.

Clues That Point to Infidelity

Following a map to the treasure chest of betrayal

Rachel didn't need a real map to find the treasure chest of breakup betrayal in her home. She used her woman's intuition to search for clues that Tony, her husband, had been cheating on her. Little things around the house seemed noticeably different and she felt something was amiss. After a while she became more and more certain that it *was* a Miss who was causing these doubts. Perhaps even a Miss Tress. And each clue bought her closer to the Treasure Chest of Breakup Betrayal.

The Tale of Rachel

Rachel was not a suspicious person by nature, but one day she came home from work and, smelling a pleasant scent in the air, picked up her dog Curry and sniffed him, just in case he had been into her hand lotion again. Negative. She lifted her arm and sniffed herself and was happy to find her new deodorant was not only working well, but gave off a scent of lily of the valley. But it wasn't the same smell as the one that lingered in the air. A nagging feeling caused her to suspect that her husband, Tony, was hiding something from her. The fragrance held the smell of scented betrayal; someone had been burning her Bordello de Paree candle and she knew it wasn't her.

Her mind traveled back to the last time she felt things weren't right. That was the day she discovered cigarette ash on the coffee table, lying there like a sausage-shaped mini volcanic eruption next to the mule that wore a sign around its neck that read "Souvenir of the Grand Canyon." When she asked Tony who had been smoking in their home, he said Kevin had visited and had smoked a cigarette or two. Rachel knew he was lying for two reasons. Firstly, Kevin hated all things smoky. In fact, he wouldn't even eat the smoked ham and cheese sandwich she made him when they all watched the Superbowl together, because the smoky flavor made him cough. Secondly, she knew her husband well enough to recognize when he was lying, because when he lied his eyebrows twitched. When Tony mentioned Kevin's name, the twitching began, first the left eyebrow, then the right, resulting in a tiny but distinct frenzied eyebrow samba.

Rachel never told him she could tell when he was lying because it was a useful tool for her, so why give up a good thing? But who had been smoking in their house and why did Tony lie?

That afternoon, she felt like something just wasn't right and it made her uneasy. A trip to the bathroom revealed two wet, blue bath towels on the floor, which was odd because Tony never left any towels on the floor. Suspicion nudged at her sixth sense as her toe nudged the towels. Feeling uneasy because she hated confrontations as much as she hated washing laundry, she called Tony into the bathroom. "Why are there two wet towels on the bathroom floor?" she questioned him as the soggy evidence bared itself unashamedly.

"Where?" asked Tony, looking everywhere but the floor.

"There." She pointed at the waterlogged towels with her toe. While Tony looked hard at them, possibly searching for an appropriate lie, Rachel stared at his eyebrows, tossing a mental coin in her mind, heads for a lie, tails for the truth.

"I don't know what you are talking about," he finally responded, with a pinch of attitude making his voice squeak a little in the corners. "I took a shower and used two towels. Now tell me this, why did you use up all of the bread yesterday? There wasn't any left to make toast."

The eyebrows were momentarily forgotten as Rachel considered that thought. She looked at him, confused. "What's this got to do with the towels?" she asked.

"Forget the towels!" he said, picking them up and handing them to her. "I was late for work because of you. I had to stop and get breakfast on the road."

"I thought we had more bread in the freezer," she said feebly, folding up the towels. "I'm sorry."

"Well that's all right then," he said as he left the room. "Only don't do it again."

It was the perfect Tony Defense Ploy. Whenever he was losing an argument or didn't have a valid response to an accusation, he would turn the tables on the accuser and make them the guilty party. In doing this to Rachel, she always ended up apologizing. This tactic was a gift he had been born with, and one he liked to use frequently so it wouldn't be wasted.

It wasn't until 3 a.m., when she woke up with a strange feeling in the pit of her stomach that she realized he had sidetracked her, and the question of the towels was still hanging in the bathroom.

A week later, Rachel was in the kitchen making a pot of green tea. As she looked into the sink, the map of suspicion in her mind made her see something she ordinarily would not have noticed. Lying in the center of the sink was a big metal X. Everyone knows all treasure maps have an "X" on them, which marks the spot where the treasure lies and her sink was no different. There lay the culinary evidence, blatant as the results from a lie-detector test. Two sets of silverware and two plates from a cooked lunch were stacked in the sink. Two greasy knives with a little potato residue lay across each other, making a large X. Probably one set of dishes was Tony's, but because he never cooked more than scrambled eggshells Rachel wondered who had cooked the meal and eaten from the other plate? She stormed into the living room, brandishing a greasy knife in her fist.

"Who cooked this meal?" she asked Tony, waving the knife in the air as a blob of wet potato slopped onto the rug. Silence. She headed back into the kitchen. After a few minutes, Tony followed her in. He watched her as she picked up the tea kettle and poured boiling water into the teapot. She turned to face him. "And who ate from the other plate?" She spooned sugar into a cup then she poured out a cup of tea for him. He took it from her. The excuse he gave her was weak and unacceptable, just like the cup of tea he was holding. The lie that came from his mouth was so far-fetched it would have put even an uncreative lying teenager to shame.

"I was really hungry," he stated feebly, "so I had two lunches." She stared at his honest eyebrows. They were twitching furiously like two mating caterpillars on a honeymoon. She turned away with her tea and didn't speak to him for the rest of the evening.

The next day would reveal everything.

The next day (the one that would reveal everything), Tony came home with a banana crème pie he said a friend at work had made for him. Even though the problems of the previous day stood like bars on a jail cell forming a barrier between them, Tony and Rachel shared the pie. It was so delicious they agreed it was the best pie they had ever tasted. It was so good they extended themselves, along with their belts, and ate it all.

Rachel decided to go to bed early that night, and as she walked into their bedroom with a bellyful of pie, she was hit with a pungent smell. The stench of cheap, unfamiliar perfume was overpowering and actually made her eyes water. Where was it coming from? On impulse, she bent down and sniffed the bed. It reeked of Eau my God, which was a perfume she despised, and she knew then, without a doubt, that there had been between-the-sheet deceit. Tony had been unfaithful.

With tears slipping off her chin, she left the sleazy-smelling bedroom and dragged herself into the living room to confront him as he watched television. She asked him three times if he had a girlfriend, and like Judas Iscariot, he denied her each time. His face was so animated with shock and emotion that it was difficult for her to establish whether he was lying or not. It was a standoff, but Rachel wasn't giving up. She stared at his face until he looked into her eyes, then he finally admitted that there was someone else. When she saw his eyebrows innocently dozing in the lamplight she knew it was the truth. Her questions and his explanations flew back and forth like a hypnotist's pocket watch as they discussed the details of their relationship, old and new, and a few bottles of red wine coursed through their brains. Finally, as dawn pushed the sun awake and daylight leaked into the room, their words were all spent and relationship changes hung in the air like a lead piñata. Rachel thought she could never forgive him.

Tony stood up to leave and to spend what was left of the night in a hotel. Suddenly he smiled at her. Through the murkiness of the red wine recently consumed, her anger melted and she smiled back at this man whom she still loved. It broke the ice and they both knew right then that no one could take away the rapport they had. Maybe she could forgive him after all.

She followed him through the kitchen, towards the back door to say goodbye. Reaching for the door handle, he momentarily hesitated and turned back around. She felt a burst of love for him as he looked into her eyes one more time. "He's going to give up his girlfriend!" she thought desperately to herself. "He still loves me!" But it was not to be. He reached over to the counter, picked up the empty banana crème pie dish and handed it to her. She gazed at it; perhaps he was giving it to her as a gift because they had both enjoyed the pie so much. Tony smiled again as he asked "Do you mind washing the pie dish before I leave? I want to be sure it's clean when I return it to my girlfriend later on today."

Rachel felt the blood move up to her face, making her hot and dizzy. His careless words reached into her body, tore out her heart and cast it down the garbage disposal. She saw the color red dancing around her eyes. How dare he ask her to wash the dish! Had she suddenly become a maid to his girlfriend? It was humiliating enough that he had encouraged her to eat a pie baked by her. The very same girl who had touched the pie dough and Tony with the same hands. The hands that reeked of Eau de Slut.

Her stomach churned a crème pie-like mixture inside her as she used the dish he had given to her to catch the partially digested pie that spewed up from her stomach like a rancid milkshake. The sickly aroma permeated the air of the room and stifled her olfactory senses. He watched as she retched, horrifically mesmerized, and when she handed the dish back to him with its fresh new contents, he took it without a word. She looked him coldly in the eye. "Now you can bring the dish back to your girlfriend," she said, "and you can tell her I saved her some pie."

Comment

Often we can overlook one or two little clues that indicate something is going on in our home with our partner, just because we want everything to be all right. Sometimes a twitch of the eyebrows speaks a thousand words of mistrust, but often it's a trail of clues that makes us suspicious. It could begin with dinner and end with pie but somewhere in-between there has to be confrontation. We may love our partner to heaven and back, but if they have someone else on their mind, usually there's little that can change that. You have to know if there's someone else, so you have The Big Talk, where you look into their cheating eyes or caterpillar eyebrows and ask if they are having a little dessert on the side you don't yet know about. If they refuse to be honest with you, at least be honest with yourself. Are you aware of clues that are adding up on the map of doubts in your mind? If so, the outcome will find us standing at the treasure chest of breakup betrayal. Unfortunately, in this case, the only bounty the chest held was something regurgitated. It was time for Rachel to follow the map back home and right out of this relationship.

Lust and Obsession
The sputtering flame of desire

You don't know what it's like if you haven't experienced it. You can't even explain it to certain people and have them fully understand how you feel. It's lust; it's an obsession, and if it happens to you outside of your relationship, it will kill it stone dead.

What is your definition of cheating? If someone in a relationship spends a lot of time with someone of the opposite sex but doesn't sleep with them, is that cheating? What if two people meet and have a quickie in a back alleyway after knowing each other for only five minutes, then never see each other again? If that is cheating, then cheating is just having sex with someone else. Is cheating the icing on the sex cake of friendship?

Sneaky sex with someone you like and meetings outside of a relationship are easy to categorize as being unfaithful, but what if your body controls your mind and demands you follow its raw, basic instinct? Can you blame nature and say, "It's the way God made me. I couldn't control my urges?" Lust lives inside the brain and is fed by what we see, what we smell, and a fundamental hormonal urge. The stepping stone from lust to cheating, is opportunity.

The Tale of Marc

Marc took the number 3 bus to work every day and always sat near the back. The first time he saw the foxy lady was in the beginning of July, when the weather began to turn steaming hot, even in the mornings. He passed by Foxy each time he made his way to his seat and it was difficult for him not to notice that she was just like the weather, steaming hot. He tried to make eye contact with her, but she never seemed to notice him. She was dark and dusky, very different from his wife, Natalie, who was blonde and fair-skinned. Thoughts of Foxy became as regular as breakfast in his life and as time went by, they grew to be as regular as every meal in his life, including snacks.

He started sitting directly behind her on the bus each morning and would stare at the back of her head adoringly. Sometimes he would lean forward and surreptitiously smell her hair and the light fragrant smell would seem to grab him below the belt with a perfumed tingle. Secretly he tried to capture her breath on his cheek as he craned his head toward her, and he breathed in the air she breathed out and he felt it enter his body and he was ecstatic. At night and all night he wondered how it would feel to kiss her and his never ending-thoughts of her would cause him to sweat a bit more on his side of the bed, making a little damp patch that he slept in.

She was an obsession and his life revolved around the 7 a.m. hour when he would see her on the bus. She took over his world and it wasn't his fault; it was an occurrence of circumstance. He felt she was the summer he had waited all winter for. As she sat in front of him with her aura all around him, Marc knew this was not enough for him. His fantasies had taken over his life and he had to know her, have her, possess her, because his life was now completely out of control. Even though she wore a wedding ring, he knew she was also attracted to him.

One bright and sticky morning he conjured up enough nerve to sit next to her. As he sat down it felt as though he had dived into a pool of icy water and he couldn't catch his breath. It took him from 18th Street to 32nd Street before his heart calmed down and he was able to say "hello" and start a conversation. Every day after that first "hello," he would sit with her on the bus and he felt sure she had feelings for him because she would hold his gaze just a little bit too long, with a look that brazenly penetrated his clothing. Their lust-ship thickened the air between them as wicked thoughts and moist looks were exchanged and Marc struggled with his suppressed infidelity. They exchanged cell phone numbers and they texted each other. He gave her a special ringtone, "Foxy Lady," and she became his laxative because each time she would text him, his stomach became so nervous that he didn't know whether to read the text or run to the bathroom. Such a lust was impossible to resist and their bodies ached for one another.

An illicit shameless affair began, where the sex was hotter than burnt toast and as sensual as warm syrup. Sadly, most lustships are very much like grenades, they explode with a bang (or many bangs, in this case); there are bright lights and fireworks and sometimes even classical music. Then everything fizzles out with a tiny fartlike sound as it ends. Dead. Marc and Foxy were ill-fated like Romeo and Juliet, but not as tragic. Their love was doomed before they even realized there was no love, only making love. But, by then, all was lost because they had confessed their unfaithfulness to their spouses. To this day Marc still can't listen to the song "Foxy Lady" without it relaxing his bowels. He was conditioned, like Pavlov's dog and that was all that remained of their lust. Thus ends the story of Marc and Foxy.

Comment

Sometimes people's fantasies grow out of control and short of leaving the country, there's little you can do except try to control those obsessive thoughts. Images of the new attraction become entwined with your feelings and suddenly normal thoughts and everyday life scuttle out the window as you live in a fantasy with your sex idol. You are making a fool of yourself with that 20 year old from the office, getting a hair weave or buying a red sports car. Or maybe you gave up your spouse for a grope in a bar but once it's over, it really is all over, including your relationship.

Obsession is a powerful motivator but it dies quickly and Marc's fixation on Foxy eventually faded. It seemed that the more he grew to know her as a person, the more he didn't like her. Poor Marc. But who knows, if his fantasies hadn't taken the obsessive route, would he have stayed with his wife anyway? Shakespeare didn't write an ending to that particular tragedy.

Departing the Relationship
Look at your watch—is it time to leave already?

The reasons for leaving your partner might be lined up like a firing squad, ready to shoot your relationship dead and put it out of its misery. While it puts on a blindfold and smokes its last cigarette, you step in like the Governor with a pardon. "Leave that relationship alone!" you command with authority. "It's not ready to die yet. We're going to give it another week."

"Not so fast," interrupts your ex, appearing on the scene twirling a loaded pistol. "I'm ready to kill it now."

You fall to your knees, there's a loud bang and when the dust clears you find yourself back at home, sleeping in the guestroom and trying to find an apartment to rent. But why shouldn't you stay in the shared home just a bit longer? After all, what's the big rush?

The Tale of Todd

It was two days after Christmas when Maggie broke up with Todd, and as she said the words, "I think we should break up," the last bite of the blueberry pancake was heading toward Todd's mouth. As every muscle in his body relaxed, his fork fell from his hand and impaled itself onto the carpet. Maggie's dog, Icon, deftly grabbed the food from the fork before it hit the target, and then sidestepped the falling dart like a kid playing chicken with a penknife. Todd wiped his mouth with the back of his hand and asked Maggie the standard questions, "Are you sure? Is there someone else? Is it something I did?" And most importantly, "What can I do to change your mind?"

"Sadly," Maggie said, "there's nothing you can do. It's over."

Todd didn't see this coming. He was an optimist and also not very observant, so he didn't realize their relationship had become as unfriendly as a beard of bees. It was only Maggie's feelings and her moods that had changed; his remained the same. So, as a consideration to Maggie, he immediately moved his things out of the master bedroom and into the guestroom. It wasn't the most cheerful of rooms, but Todd pushed away the storage boxes to make a tall stack in the corner, while Icon helped by cleaning away the spider's webs with his nose. Todd decorated the room with his books and photographs of Maggie, and his bicycle leaned against the wall like a lazy old friend.

The end of the year was just around the bend and Todd could already see it packing its bags in his mind's eye, getting ready to leave to make space for the new one—just as Todd should have been doing, but wasn't. Todd continued his life like nothing had happened and remained in their shared home, because he still believed Maggie would take him back. Sleeping in the guestroom was the only change he made, and instead of his bed harboring a soft-skinned, pleasant smelling woman, he now shared it with a wirehaired, snoring beastie with dog breath. Maggie was rarely at home so the two bachelors, Todd and Icon became inseparable, with Todd seeking out Icon when he was feeling lonely, and Icon following Todd around like an orphaned child.

The week between Christmas and New Year went slowly by and then, quick as a February snowstorm, New Year's Eve came just when expected. Todd had no social plans for that evening but felt sure Maggie would spend that hallowed night with him and Icon. This might be the night she would relent and take him back. He had bought snacks for everyone and three bottles of Maggie's favorite sparkling white wine to bribe her, or rather, to bring in the New Year with her, but unfortunately Maggie had plans of her own. Her family was hosting a New Year's Eve party and she spent the early part of the evening walking around the house in various forms of dress and undress in preparation for the party. Once sufficiently beautified, she wished Todd a good night, kissed Icon on his doglike cheek and disappeared into the chilly night.

The slam of the door was like a stake through Todd's heart, but it was also his signal to prepare for his own New

Year's Eve celebrations. Icon followed him into the kitchen and watched him defrost some seasonal frozen snacks to share, which may or may not have been pigs in blankets and sliders. Looking back, he could never remember what he ate that night, but Icon would always remember; the memory of real beef in the sliders and unknown animal parts in the hot dogs haunting his food memory bank for the rest of his canine life.

Todd watched a couple of movies that night but avoided the New Year's Eve celebrations on the television, because he wasn't ready to give up the old year yet, along with all of its memories. The evening passed quickly and he and Icon dozed cheek to cheek, content with a bellyful of oven-heated treats. When the phone rang at 12:10 a.m., Todd was suddenly wide-awake and booze and happiness flowed through his veins because he knew it would be Maggie, because she would never forget him.

"Hi!" he said brightly, into the phone, the white wine making his speech a little slurred.

"Happy New Year!" came Maggie's voice in response.

"Same to you," said Todd, trying to sit up and not spill his wine over the dog. "How's the family?"

"Very well," answered Maggie, "in fact there's someone here who would like to say Happy New Year to you," she said. "I'll just pass them over."

"Happy New Year, Todd," boomed a man's voice. Todd tried to place the voice. Uncle Bob? Cousin Alex? Maggie's father? That was it. Marty, the old devil himself.

"Happy New Year to you, too!" said Todd as the man put Maggie back on the phone. "Your dad sounds good," he said to Maggie. "He seems quite sober this time."

"Oh, dad's fine," replied Maggie, "but that wasn't dad. That was my new boyfriend, Colin," she explained. "When I told him you were spending New Year's Eve alone he felt sorry for you. He's such a sweet guy. He wanted to call and wish you a happy New Year."

Have you ever had the feeling you are floating up by the ceiling and watching yourself sitting pathetically on the couch with a nervous dog on your lap? Listening to Maggie's words, Todd had a brief out-of-body experience, but then a shriek of anguish came from his mouth that brought him back down again. It was so piercing even he himself was unable to hear it, but he felt his lips move. Icon heard the shriek as it was on the dog frequency level, and immediately all of the neighborhood canines who lived within a one mile radius were barking and howling. As Todd slammed down the phone and jumped up, he spilled his wine over Icon, who instinctively sprang into action. But it didn't take Maggie's dog to bite Todd on the ankle to sober him up, he was already stone cold sober. At 12:15 a.m. on January 1st, Todd knew within seconds he would be moving out of his shared home with Maggie to stay with his sister Carly. In fact, it would be right after he bandaged the dog bite on his ankle, but before he got a rabies shot. It was never too soon to leave.

Comment

Todd wouldn't accept that his New Year's goose was cooked and it was time to turn off the oven, finish up the baked snacks and move out. He needed something like a stick of dynamite under the couch cushion to help him make the decision to leave Maggie, but a phone call and a dog bite turned out to be just as helpful. Sometimes, initially, it's easier to remain in a relationship that has ended, but it really only delays the heartbreak. Once the relationship has sunk to the bottom of the water and you can't ignore that fact any longer, then you have to move on—and move out. If you stay like an unwelcome guest, don't be expecting free meals or sympathy. Staying will only make you look like you are in denial, or lazy, or just happy to have central heat when it's snowing outside.

If you are hoping they will take you back you may be delusional. If you think they will take you back after seeing you sit around the house long enough, you are wrong. In fact, if you sit around too long, you may end up like the rarely-used piece of exercise equipment people have in their basement that they hang their laundry on to dry. After a while, its original use is forgotten. Don't end up as your ex's clothes hanger, because you are too good for that. Of course it's easier to sit tight, close your eyes and hope everything turns back to normal, but you need a genie in a lamp to fix that for you, or a witch's potent spell.

After the goodbyes are all said, it's time for someone to make an exit and at certain times, that someone should be you. Pack your bags and fill your head with dignity as you stride out of the home that is no longer yours. It can often take a prod to encourage you to move out. Sometimes, like Todd, you need a wirehaired hound nipping at your ankles to chase you out the door.

Suspicious Mates
Snipping the umbilical cord of jealousy

People experience jealousy in different degrees. For some it's like being jostled in the subway; it's confrontational, but ends quickly after they say, "I'm sorry. I didn't mean to touch your girlfriend's behind. It was just something soft to brace myself against when the train stopped short." For others, it's a threadbare electric blanket worn around the shoulders, ready to zap them at their first sign of jealousy. Everyone needs some space in their relationships, but where do you draw the line between letting your partner live their life and wondering if they are having too much fun without you?

We all feel jealous sometimes. The feeling comes on rapidly and can make you feel as though a couple of gremlins are running around your guts, feeding your insides tranquilizers and jumping up and down on your stomach. You are nervous and angry and the only cure is reassurance or separation from the cause. But dwelling on it will push you over the edge of the excessive jealousy cliff, right into the mouth of a waiting divorce attorney.

The Tale of Jake

Jake was happy in his relationship with Donna, but Donna had no time for happiness. Every moment in her life was colored green and it wasn't because she was Irish. It was the little green devil of jealousy who sat on her shoulder like the anti-Cupid, looking to shoot a poisoned arrow at any sign of happiness coming her way. Her jealousies caused her to suffer physically. Her eyes stared, she became hot and clammy and her heart raced. Her only remedy was to believe Jake when he denied her accusations of infidelity, because if she didn't, the jealousy heated up from the inside out, like soup cooked in a microwave.

She monitored his phone calls, his errands, and every activity he undertook when he was not with her. She called him at work, at his mother's, and at the football game, where she asked to speak to his friends to make sure he was really with them. He tried hard to reassure her that he wasn't playing around, just merely out with the guys, but she wouldn't believe him. One night he was awakened by the dog sniffing in his ear with bursts of hot breath. Only it wasn't the dog, it was Donna who was smelling his hair to find out where he had been, trying to sniff out the scent of unfaithfulness. His new nickname for her became Bloodhound.

Each day she demanded his cell phone and each day he would hand it to her, waiting, standing at ease while she checked it—the General checking her troops. Once she was satisfied there were no calls or texts from strangers, she would hand it back to him with a burning unspoken suspicion that he might have another phone hidden away somewhere.

Donna's suspicions finally came to a head one evening when Jake told her he was going to visit a client. He had only been driving for a few moments when he noticed Donna was surreptitiously following him in her car. He wondered what she was up to, so he began to drive slowly so that she could keep up. He led her on a useless trail, over rivers on narrow bridges; into areas where windows and doors were locked because crime was high and then deeper into areas where windows and doors were locked and locked again, because crime there was even higher. He drove through the countryside where sheep and cows stopped their munching and stared as they both cruised by. He traveled down city streets thick with taxis and heavy with rush hour and still she followed him like Hansel and Gretel following the trail of breadcrumbs to the witch's house. Jake called his client while he drove, to reschedule their meeting to another day, and after that he called his friend Gary and told him what was happening, and between them they concocted a prank to catch Donna out.

After an hour and a half of driving aimlessly around, with Donna still following close behind, Jake finally turned into Gary's street and parked his car outside his friend's house. Moments later, Donna arrived and parked where she thought Jake couldn't see her. She watched him leave his car and walk toward a house. When he rang the bell a woman answered the door. She was blonde and from what Donna could see, she was buxom and wearing a heavy robe. She put her arms around Jake and they appeared to be kissing. With some urgency they went into the house together, their arms still wrapped around each other and slammed the door behind them.

Donna left her car and crept toward a large oak tree that stood across from the house Jake was visiting. She hid under its branches, holding her breath to see what would happen next. Looking at the house, she saw an upstairs light come on and a shadow pulled sheer curtains across the window. Another shadow joined the first and they began kissing.

Then, to Donna's horror, they started removing their clothes. She knew it! She had known all along he was being unfaithful to her and now she had caught him with his other woman. She wondered how many girlfriends he had and what other kinds of skullduggery he was up to.

A streetlight flickered and failed over Donna's head and as she looked up, the oak tree reached out a branch and grabbed her hair. Giving a little cry, she elbowed the branch into submission and furiously disentangled her hair. She marched up to the house and rapped on the door, calling "Come out Jake! I know you're in there. I can see you through the window." Footsteps sounded on the stairs and fear caused her sweat glands to work double overtime. The door slowly opened and a man stood before her, holding a knife in one hand that dripped blood onto the tiled floor. In his other hand was Jake's striped shirt that she had seen him wearing only a few minutes ago. It was stained in blood.

"Oh my God!" she cried out.

"You're next!" yelled the man with the knife and lunged at Donna. By the time she had reached her car, her heart was pounding, ready to explode and blood rushed through her ears, a whooshing river of heat. She drove away with the brakes screaming and she screamed along with them— a duet of automobile feedback. Fear pressed hard on the gas pedal and dust flew around behind her, reminiscent of a high-speed car chase in the movies. As she glanced in her rear view mirror she could see the murderer standing in the doorway, shaking his knife at her. He was laughing an evil and gruesome laugh and her body became ice from head to toe.

She drove north recklessly for about ten minutes then realized that she was only another five minutes from home. How could that be? It took them at least an hour and a half to reach Jake's lover's house. Logic told her they must have been driving around in circles, but panic made her a disbeliever of that theory. When she reached their house, to her relief, Jake's car was already parked outside and she ran in.

"Jake! Jake! Are you there?" she called out in desperation.

"Yes, I'm here," responded Jake calmly, turning down the volume on the television. "My client canceled so I just came home." He looked her over. "You're as white as a ghost!" he exclaimed. "Where have you been?"

Once everything had been explained, Donna never spoke directly to Jake ever again, only through her attorney. It didn't matter that Jake apologized for setting her up. He and his friend Gary had orchestrated the whole plot with props from last year's Halloween party, including the Marilyn Monroe wig that Gary wore when he played the part of Jake's girlfriend at the window, along with the fake blood. Jake later heard that Donna never dated again. Her trust in all men had been forever murdered.

Comment

Suspicion and jealousy are closely-linked emotions where the individuals make their own rules, so it's much like cheating at cards. Unfortunately, emotions don't come with guidelines so it can be difficult to know what's reasonable and what's not. Like a cat running away on a whim, our determination to find the truth also cannot be stopped, especially once our jealousies have heard the starting pistol. Once we begin distrusting someone, it's similar to rage—difficult to control once it has been started, and that's why the phrase "jealous rage" was created. Is there an antidote for out-of-control jealousy? Yes there is and its name is Trust, which can be gained by giving your partner space, believing them, or else starting fresh with someone new.

But Donna made her bond with Jake a relationship death wish from the very beginning. Her fear of losing him was so fanatical, that unconsciously she looked for a way to bring it about. In cases like this, someone will always fall to the ground grasping their chest, and it doesn't have to be the person who is being stabbed, or their wife. Everyone needs space in a relationship, even Siamese twins.

Falling Out of Love
It's more interesting watching paint dry

We hear stories of cheating, lying, money problems, abuse, but how often do we hear the banal "I just didn't love him anymore?" It's a boring statement, not juicy and scandalous like the other reasons people leave each other. Stories about loss of love are boring.

"What happened between you and Sal?"

"We fell out of love."

"Oh really? I hear we are getting some snow later on today."

Unless there's a homicide, or illicit sex, it's just not interesting.

Falling out of love shows a gap in the relationship's harmonious balance. Everyone wants their life to be harmonious. We like a balance in our wines; harmony in our music, and we even have a musical instrument called a harmonica, which used to be featured frequently in the old black and white films. Those movies would show a guy on death row weeping silently, while in the next cell, Red, his best friend and mass murderer played the harmonica the day before his execution. Drama isn't what it used to be, especially when filmed in color. There's nothing like black and white to show starkness and despondency. Falling out of love or becoming bored with your partner is like a film shot in color. It can lack desperation and drama.

The Tale of John

John and Victoria were childhood sweethearts. They had grown up together from sand pits to zits, from enjoyment to employment. They married at 21, had 2.0 children and had lived together for almost 25 years when Vicky decided to shatter John's aging heart by leaving him. When he asked her why she would do something like that after all the years they had been together she replied, "I just don't love you anymore. I'm done," and that was that.

John was baffled. He had become used to the monotony of routine marriage and couldn't see why it had to end just because she didn't love him anymore. He didn't know if he loved her either, but what difference did it make? But Vicky had known for a long time that they were growing apart and she was bored. It mattered to her that their marriage was unstimulating and their laughter together had dried up. She wanted out. Their routines grated on her nerves. For example, when they went out to eat that's all they did—eat. There was no longer any conversation besides "red or white? Fish or meat? Cheesecake or fruit?" Other diners in the restaurant would look the other way because they felt sorry for them.

Despite the boredom, they ate out often because home dining was even more tedious. After they finished eating, they would sit together at the table for a while, silently digesting their food. John would whistle low and tunelessly between his teeth and Vicky stared at the patterns on the wallpaper, if there were any. One evening, after soup and fish, with their dessert just a heavy ball of cheesecake in their stomachs and their words used up a decade ago, a child walked up to them and stared. He was puzzled by the trance-like quality of their demeanor, and after gazing at them for a minute or so, he approached John and tried to push him over. After a smack from his mother and before he received forgiveness from his father, they asked him why he would do such a thing.

"I thought they were cardboard cutouts," he explained. "They weren't moving. They didn't look alive."

The sad story of John and Vicky was a common one. They had spent 25 years together, which is about a third of someone's entire lifetime. Other couples they knew were married for 30, 40 even 50 years. What happened to John and Vicky? Why did Vicky become bored?

Comment

It's a known fact that back in the olde days, when many words had a superfluous "e" tacked onto the end of them, Tommy Marriage invented matrimony, or so the old wives' tale goes. In those days, marriages were short because medicine was not yet highly developed and people died young from ailments we can cure these days, like the flu, food poisoning and boils on the posterior. Marriages back then lasted perhaps 10 to 15 years (like a prison sentence with time off for good behavior), and some would agree that still might be the ideal amount of time to stay in a relationship with the same person.

It's likely people were glad to die young back then, because there was nothing to do at night. How many evenings could the wife listen to her husband complain that his shirt never had the same whiteness again after being washed in the river so many times? And how long could the husbands listen to their wives gossip about the sales at Ye Olde Shopping Malle? Nowadays people are living through to their 80's and can therefore have 50-60 married years together. Just look at how much we change every decade. Who can keep up with all of that change? Five or six decades—that's a lot of years of being nice to that same special someone! No wonder the divorce rate is 40-50 percent.

So when John asked Vicky "where is the love?" she answered, "It wore itself out."

As we age, we change; and if we embrace those changes, we allow ourselves to grow spiritually. In fact, there is a strong theory that people change quite dramatically every seven years. If we let those changes go by without acting on them, we are most likely settled in our lives and possibly complacent.

But you are growing and liking things you never liked before and becoming bored with things you thought were better than fast food just seven years or so ago. Your partner is growing too, and if you are moving in the same direction, you are lucky. To expect our direction to remain the same as our partner's is like expecting tree branches to grow to the same length, which of course they don't. Some follow the sun outward; just like some of us would prefer to move to another town or follow an opportunity into another life-style. Other branches prefer to stay sheltered and warm by the trunk near the food and water supply; the way some of us enjoy a fireplace, a TV dinner and the same spouse forever. The two pieces of the jigsaw puzzle that emanated from "I do" might have graduated into "I don't fit together with you anymore." And do you know what happens when you try to force those two odd pieces together? The whole damn puzzle rises in the middle and the pieces fly all over the place, then the dog runs off with some of them and you have to get a new partner.

Being Caught Out
Animal cunning goes awry

Sexual desire can get you into all kinds of trouble unless it's properly contained inside a relationship. It's a bit like keeping fire ants in a closed box. Often people are very careful in hiding their lustful extra marital relationships, but more often than not, people just *think* they are being very careful in hiding them. These are people who were probably no good at hide and go seek when they were young. They think if they close their eyes, no one can see them fooling around.

The Tale of Carlene

Carlene was a stay-at-home mother and had always trusted Tim, her bespectacled husband, who had the innocent look of a lamb and the heart of a Dickens' scoundrel. When Tim said he was working late, why should Carlene disbelieve him? She was a small-town girl whose mama had always respected the men in her family and she had raised her daughters to be the same. Carlene and Tim were like a couple of love birds and their relationship was strong, like a bull. Carlene spent her days at home with the children, and like a mother hen, she loved it. She took care of the house, the meals and the household bills and made sure everyone was looked after. She had two children, a college degree and was also street smart, so she had made herself the best of all worlds.

The second story within the story was that Tim had another life as well as his happily married one. It was only a part-time life, not like the real one with Carlene, but it was a pleasant diversion for him to be away from the wife and kids from time to time. He had furnished himself with a girlfriend to while away the hours between family and work because television didn't interest him and he had no hobbies. Tim had small delusions of grandeur, which may sound like a contradiction, and may also be one, but because of his secret second life he thought himself as sly as a fox and as handsome as a peacock. Or at least that's what his girlfriend Isobel told him.

Their usual routine was to meet at Isobel's apartment every Tuesday evening, and Tim told Carlene he had to work overtime each Tuesday evening, so he didn't have to keep thinking up new lies.

One Tuesday morning, Tim decided to skip work and he called Isobel to let her know that he had reserved a room for them at the Shady Tryst Hotel for their rendezvous, to celebrate their one-year anniversary of philandering. The hotel required Tim to provide a credit card number in order to secure the room until he arrived, but Tim, ever as devious as a scorpion had paid cash once he checked in, so that his wife Carlene would not see any charges on their joint credit card statement.

After a day of wild monkey sex with Isobel, Tim ordered pizza to the room and they drank cheap sparkling wine and watched a movie until 10 p.m. Isobel stayed overnight and while she slept, Tim crept out of the room silently as a tiger stalking its prey, so as not to awaken her. Arriving at the marital home, Tim stealthily slunk into bed smoothly as a snake shedding its skin as his wife Carlene slept, innocent as a lamb.

It was only one week later that Tim found out he wasn't as wily as he thought he was. In fact, this time he was as dumb as an ox. Carlene opened the mail every day and Overtime Tuesdays were no exception. This Tuesday, however, a surprise fee had appeared on their joint credit card bill and Carlene was determined to lock horns with Tim over it. At around 11 p.m. that evening, Tim crept soundlessly as a stag into his home and before he had closed the front door, Carlene swooped down on him, waving the offending credit card bill at him like an angry magpie flapping its wings to chase off an invading cuckoo from its nest.

"What the fox is this?" she accused him. "What is this hotel charge on our credit card bill for last Wednesday night at the Shady Tryst Hotel?" Now Tim may have thought that he was a smart man, but he was never quick thinking on his feet and not always the brightest firefly in the jar. This time was no exception. He spoke before he thought.

"That can't be right," he answered her quickly, like a greyhound running the last lap home. "We stayed there on Tuesday night, not on Wednesday night and anyway, I paid cash for the room." That remark was about to render him as dead as a dodo.

"What do you mean, 'we stayed there on Tuesday night' and you paid cash for the room?" Carlene roared, her leonine face an open page to her rage.

Tim looked at her sheepishly, afraid to utter any more incriminating words. Suffice to say that was not a good night for Tim Bird, and he was in the doghouse for many weeks to come. But why was there a charge on his credit card for Wednesday night? It turned out that Isobel had been sleeping like a hibernating bear and didn't wake up until late that morning. She dressed at a snail's pace and missed the 12 noon checkout deadline, so the hotel charged for an extra night the only way they knew how—on Tim's credit card. So Wily the Fox turned out to be caught in a trap of his own making. Snafued!

Comment

The moral of the story is you have to keep your ducks in a row when you are telling lies. It may be a bit clichéd to say that Tim was a cheetah, but another word also applies to him. It means over-confident and implies a person who thinks he knows everything. That word is "cocksure." Enough said.

Mentally Cheating
Can cheating only in your head make you mental?

an you cheat, but only in your head? Is a fantasy about someone other than your spouse mentally cheating? Compare it to committing a crime that you never get caught for—is it still a crime if you are not found out, or if no one ultimately gets hurt? It's like the age-old question, if a tree falls in a forest does it make a sound if no one is there to hear it? If not, can it cause damage? Yes it can if it falls onto your car.

The Tale of Debbie

Debbie and Oscar had a healthy marriage. They shared the chores, they shared the cooking and they even took turns on "who's on top tonight?" But Debbie was jealous because she believed that Oscar had fantasies about other women. Whenever they went out he would stare at women as they walked by and sometimes he would even smile at them and try to engage them in small talk. It was as if he was required to give his attention to every female he saw, even the old ladies buying antacids at the drug store. Age didn't matter to him; he was as equally attentive to a young woman as he was to an old one. "I'm just being friendly," he would say to Debbie, but she was certain he was obsessed by women and she considered that to be mentally cheating. It was the same when he saw a woman on the television. He was compelled to make a comment about how attractive she was and it would tug at her heartstrings when they made love because she would always wonder who he was thinking about while they were together.

One Monday evening, Oscar brought home a cabinet from his storage unit that he had from his bachelor days, thinking they could use a nice piece of heavy furniture somewhere in the house. It fitted perfectly just below the window in the master bedroom. It was more than a little dusty and Debbie wiped it down with wood polish and placed a vase of dried flowers on top. It really was a good looking piece of furniture.

It was two weeks later when Debbie was admiring the intricate, carved design on the doors that depicted a nine point shell with flowers and leaves around it, that she noticed the center door wasn't quite closed. The corner of a magazine was sticking out that was preventing it from closing all the way. She opened the door to stuff it back in. She saw that other magazines were stacked in there, and as she pushed the stray one back in, an abstract pattern of globular objects on the cover of one of the magazines caught her eye. They were artistically displayed like fruit in a bowl—for a party, perhaps—and at first she thought they were cookery magazines.

The objects seemed to be intertwined with one another and the picture gave the same symmetrical feel that a child's kaleidoscope gives when you look through the viewing window.

She pulled out the publication and for a second the whirling circles hypnotized her and she couldn't quite place what they were, but they certainly looked familiar. Then they came into focus she realized that they were breasts. Women's breasts and there were lots of them. There must be three or four women on the cover of this magazine, thought Debbie, all with their tops off. Why would they all take their tops off? Maybe they were on vacation and it was hot. But they seemed to be laying all over each other. How bizarre.

For a moment she stared, still not knowing the whys and wherefores and then it hit her. Pornography. She had never seen it before and the women really did have all of their clothes off. Having removed the first magazine from the cabinet and disturbing the delicate balance of the stacks of the magazines inside, a floodgate of porn opened up into the bedroom, and a windfall of magazines came tumbling out like a Las Vegas slot machine jackpot with nudity as the prize. There seemed to be hundreds of them. Not only magazines, but also DVD's with cover art of nudity, like an out of control anatomy class.

Debbie had never seen pictures like these before, not even in a National Geographic magazine. She picked up one of the magazines that had fallen onto her lap and out of curiosity she looked at the pages. She was fascinated. The people in these magazines were doing all manner of things with not only each other, but also with gadgets and objects, and everyone was smiling. What fun they seemed to be having! Suddenly the bedroom door clicked open, pulling Debbie out of her reverie and the hard world of reality tapped her on the shoulder.

"What's going on here?" asked Oscar, as he tapped her on the shoulder.

"I might ask you the same question," responded a red-faced and stammering Debbie. "Look what I found in the cabinet. It's disgusting," she added, clearly embarrassed. "Who keeps such things? And look how many!" Oscar was at a loss for words. "Oops" seemed too small for the situation and a curse word might have matched the scene too appropriately.

"Those are all old things I had before I met you. I thought that I had thrown them out," he ventured. "I don't like things like this anymore. I forgot that they were in there." Debbie shivered. The unintentional damage had been done.

Sadly, this proved to Debbie that he had been unfaithful to her. He had been cheating with the women in these magazines and maybe real women, too. Probably also with those online women from Sweden and Russia whose ads appeared in her email spam folder from time to time. Those women were really persistent and their spelling was horrendous.

She ran into the bathroom crying, and no apologizing from Oscar could bring her out. What if he was thinking about other women when they were making love together? Surely after looking at all of those women, the images must still be dancing in his head like sugarplums in the Christmas verse. Or probably crawling all over him and each other in his mind's eye. That was definitely mentally cheating, which was just as bad as real cheating. If the intent was there, the possibilities were endless.

The next day they had The Talk and Debbie accused him of mentally cheating. Oscar understood how that term might apply to him, but he knew that he was guiltless in the cheating field.

"There's no such thing," he said to her. "Cheating is about touching and feeling and giving up your mind and body to someone else. I am happy with you and I don't want anyone else." But Debbie believed the dirty deed was just around the corner, leaning on a lamp on a street corner and smoking a pre-coital cigarette. She felt betrayed and couldn't come to terms with his behavior. She was sure that when they made love, he was picturing someone else; someone with glossy skin, airbrushed extremities and coiffed girlie parts.

A break up was inevitable and Oscar was glad he had kept his cabinet of porn. On those cold and lonely winter nights in his bachelor apartment he was never alone; he had Jessie Juggs and Bambi Stroker to keep him company. As for Debbie, she firmly believed Oscar's mental cheating had broken them up. Of course such a thing exists, she reasoned to herself. Shouldn't she be the object of his desire, and not some unknown female who may or may not have enhanced parts? But she couldn't stay with him. Paranoid, or not? Unreasonable, or not? Mentally cheating, or not?

Comment

No one likes sexual competition and it's as difficult to compete with magazine or online models as it is to lure away your gay attractive friend from someone of the same sex. If talking about this situation cannot solve it, issuing an ultimatum to your partner might work—the old "it's them or me" threat. On the other hand, it may also force your partner to be secretive about their pastimes as they continue with mentally cheating behind your back. Or is there no such thing?

Should Oscar have been more sensitive to Debbie's uncertainties? He could have been less honest and hidden his shiny little secrets, applying the adage of "ignorance is bliss." After all, who wants to think their lover is picturing other people instead of you while you are naked and trying to be sexy? But let's be fair to Oscar. Perhaps Debbie was also in his fantasies along with a couple or three of those air-brushed women. However, if he told her that, it might have given Debbie something else to worry about, and like the rest of us, she has her own insecurities. She believed she had to move on. Was she being extreme or was she just jealous? If so, of whom? Of someone Oscar had never met? Someone who might be 20 years older now or in a retirement home? Someone who was nothing but a fantasy? Debbie wanted 100% of her man, physically and mentally. It's not unnatural to want this unless you say it out loud and someone hears you… and then it begins to sound somewhat excessive.

Piecing Together the Puzzle of a Breakup
Harder than gluing a mosaic vase

When racehorses are given blinkers to wear during a race, it stops them from looking around and being distracted. That way they concentrate only on what's ahead and they are not wondering if the grass on the left-hand side of the track is greener than the grass on the right-hand side of the track as they race along. In a failing relationship, it's very similar. Maybe you are wondering if the grass is greener on the other side, or in other words, would Hank be a better lover than Frank? But if Frank doesn't already notice that you and Hank are in the process of finding out, Frank is wearing breakup blinkers and cannot see the signs of impending separation all around him. And that's a horse of a different color.

The Tale of Frank

Frank and Wendy had an on-again-off-again dating relationship, but once they shacked up together it was on-again all the way. Wendy was a mite brighter than Frank, who was known at work as being one of the dullest knives in the drawer, but he was popular with his workmates and they rarely made fun of him anymore. But like a racehorse wearing blinkers, Frank saw only what was straight ahead of him, and he didn't see the breakup signs that suddenly became visible all around him. He was suffering from Classic Blinker's Disorder. See how many signs you can detect in the story below that indicate a breakup might be in the cards.

One evening Wendy came into the bathroom just as Frank was soaping himself in the shower. She asked him if he wanted to go out with her; she already had her coat on. "I just got in the shower," he responded. "You have terrible timing. Half an hour before or after and I would have gone with you." But was her timing terrible, or was it just perfect?

Later in the week when she came home from an evening out with "the girls," Wendy didn't speak to Frank. Instead, she headed for the shower, barely looking him in the eye. What could she have been doing that would make her so dirty that she needed to shower right away, he wondered? Maybe she fell down in the mud. But then why didn't she look at him or say, "hello?" It was as though she was ashamed. Why? What had she done? Then Frank decided it was because he hadn't washed his hair in a few days and she was disgusted. Or maybe he had spinach in his teeth. He headed for the bathroom and grabbed his toothbrush.

Teeth gleaming, he wandered into the kitchen and found a bakery box on the counter. He cut the string and opened it up and inside was a large chocolate cupcake in the shape of a heart, whose frosting read "Hank loves Wendy." Frank was puzzled and thought about this for a minute or two because it didn't make any sense. The name on the cake was clearly not "Frank." Then he realized that "Hank" was supposed to be "Hunk," a new loving nickname Wendy had thought up for him. It only looked like Hank because the letter U was accidentally joined at the top and smudged on one side. How sweet of her. It was his favorite too, white cake with choco-late frosting. Frank was wiping the remains of the chocolate frosting off his mouth as Wendy entered the kitchen. She seemed strangely angry that he ate the cupcake that she had bought for him. Maybe she wanted to be there when he found it. Maybe it was because he didn't save her any.

She angrily disappeared back into the bathroom, this time with her cellphone. Frank could hear her whispering into the phone, but couldn't catch what she was saying. He wondered why she was whispering and when the call ended he asked her. "I can't tell you," she said. Frank smiled at her. She was so cute! She was obviously planning a surprise for his birthday which was three short months away. He was such a lucky man!

That night in bed he made a move toward her and she shuddered and moved away from him. He decided she must be tired after her night out and he turned over to go to sleep. Late into the night her phone rang and she sprang out of bed to answer it. "Who is it?" he asked her. She covered the mouthpiece and answered, "Salesman," and walked out the bedroom door with the phone. He had always told her that she was too polite to strangers on the phone. If he happened to catch a salesman calling him at home, he would tell him to stop calling, but Wendy was the opposite with her politeness, especially when Hank the insurance salesman called. They already had insurance through a different company and Frank kept telling him to stop calling, but Wendy was too polite to hurt his feelings. Whenever she ran for the phone and it was Hank, he often heard her setting up meetings between him and her friends so they could buy insurance, as she often said things like "Tuesday evening at 8 p.m. The Bonneville Motel." What other person was as compassionate and caring as she was? "Don't be long," he called out as the bedroom door closed behind her.

The following evening Frank arrived home at 10 p.m. after working late, to find that Wendy was having a party for her friends at their house and he hadn't been invited. Frank was initially angry and questioned her on it. She replied irritably, "It's only a Tupperware party for my girlfriends." He looked around and saw quite a few men there. Hmmmm, he thought, she must have invited her gay friends too. He had heard they were excellent cooks. Oh, and look—there was Hank the insurance salesman. He was probably selling all kinds of policies to her friends. "Good party!" said Frank to a group of guys swilling beer. "Buy much Tupperware? They just smiled and nodded. "Great!" he replied.

How many clues of a breakup did you find? If you found less than three, you may not be as perceptive as you thought. If you found more than nine, you're just paranoid.

Comment

Wendy was beginning to lead a single life and Frank couldn't see that their relationship had fallen like a Shrove Tuesday pancake. Maybe he was purposely avoiding the issue by living in denial. When people look back on a broken relationship it's easy to have missed some of the signs that indicate things are beginning to go wrong. Suddenly, it's "how could I have not seen that?" or "Aha! That's why she always opened her mail in the basement!" You can't fault yourself for not seeing some of the signs, but you can give yourself a little kick on the backside if you missed them all. It's a matter of piecing together portions of your ex-partner's behavior in order to see the entire picture. Sometimes an outsider can see what's going on before you can. It's rather like gluing back together your favorite mosaic vase from Greece after it was dropped on the kitchen floor. It takes a friend to tell you that it's much too broken to try and fix.

Once your relationship has slowed down to a halt and you have put together as many clues of the impending breakup as you can, you can metaphorically take them and bury them deep in the garden. Maybe they will grow into an Awareness Bush and you can make smart soup with the leaves so that next time you'll find yourself more insightful. Or at the very least, it may increase your motor skills at completing puzzles.

Signs You Need to Move Out
A list of scenarios, myths and truths

eep in your heart you know things are getting worse between yourself and your partner, but is it really time to move out? When something happens that should make you suspicious, do you brush it under the rug and say, "I'm overreacting?" Take a look at the floor beneath your rug. Is it full of BS?

Scenario: She goes out with "friends" every night.
Myth: They are taking meals on wheels to housebound elderly people.
Truth: She is either out with a man or out to catch a man. The clue to the truth is the alcohol on her breath; the scent of sex in her hair or seeing the enticement laced across her teeth when she smiles.

Scenario: He stays in bed all through every weekend or sleeps on the couch all day.
Myth: He was bitten by a tsetse fly while vacationing in Florida and now has sleeping sickness.

Truth: Tsetse flies live in Africa, so that is unlikely. He is more likely depressed and doesn't know what to do. Sleeping is his way of switching himself off and avoiding his partner.

Scenario: They argue all of the time.
Myth: Everyone argues.
Truth: Not that much!

Scenario: There are hang ups on the house phone when he answers it.
Myth: Someone just got a new phone number that's very similar to theirs.
Truth: It's her boyfriend calling her.

Scenario: He spies on her and keeps charts of where she goes.
Myth: He is worried that she may get lost because they can't afford a GPS.
Truth: He thinks she is having an affair.

Scenario: She doesn't want him to go out without her.
Myth: She loves him so much she wants to spend every minute with him.
Truth: It's because she doesn't trust him.

Scenario: He hopes she goes out every night.
Myth: He only wants her to be happy.
Truth: His girlfriend is coming over and he wants his partner out of the way.

Scenario: Someone else's toiletries are in the bathroom when he returns from a business trip.
Myth: She surprised him with a gift of new toiletries.
Truth: She had her boyfriend staying over.

Scenario: A new attractive roommate of the opposite sex has unexpectedly moved in.
Myth: They really needed some extra cash and a roommate could help.
Truth: He moved her replacement right in.

Scenario: She reads about their breakup on a social network website or a blog.
Myth: It's a practical joke.
Truth: It's the truth. The heartless truth.

PART TWO

THE RELATIONSHIP GHOST LINGERS ON

A Shot of Raw Emotions, Pity Sex and Ex-Talk

Waking Up Alone
Smacked upside the head with the breakup stick

Have you ever woken up in the morning uncomfortably aware that sweat was layered on your body and feeling tacky like the cheap white glue they use in kindergarten? You lie there counting the pink gum spitballs on the ceiling and suddenly it hits you that you're not at home. So then where are you? Your only hope is that you have been kidnapped, because God knows, this can't be where you live.

As you sit up in bed a headache punches you right in the ear, causing a ringing in the head, and it's not the kind that calls you to church on Sundays. The windshield wipers of truth sweep away the fog of sleep. There is only one thing it could be. You had been smacked upside the head with the breakup stick and this is the beginning of your new life alone.

Some lucky souls may leave their beds on the first day alone in a new place and stand by their kitchen window after their breakup, take a deep breath of rotting garbage and cheerfully say, "I am so glad I'm out of that relationship." But Lynda was not one of those people—yet. She was still to bear the burden of missing the man who had swindled her out of anything of value, with his sweet talking and convincing lies. It would be later that morning when she would find out the small, insignificant set of items she had taken from the marital home would set her on her way to forgetting him.

The Tale of Lynda

Lynda climbed out of bed into her new unfamiliar world that looked so much better when she signed her deposit check there, three weeks ago. It was true what they said about moonlight, it made everything romantic; even a cheap apartment. And this morning, daylight was not her friend. It was her first morning of living there all alone, while Chad remained in their original home. She fleetingly wondered if she had lost the coin toss for the marital home because Chad had used a two-headed dime. Being street-savvy was not one of her strong points, but at the time, he had convinced her that it was a fair way to divide up the property. Maybe she wouldn't live here for long. Maybe hell would freeze over and Chad would take her back.

She stood at the carpet's edge between bedroom and hallway, toes repelling something sticky in the course fibers. Caught in limbo as her two lifestyles crossed like red and black wires in a circuit, her old life fizzled out and the new one gained power. She walked the four steps it took to be in the center of her new kitchen. Yesterday, in the far-distant past it had taken several more steps to be in the middle of that culinary oasis. She looked around her at a neglected kitchen that a prior tenant had hurriedly excused himself from, and then she broke down and cried.

"Where is my big, beautiful, kitchen?" she demanded of the thin, grimy, fat-splatted walls whose pockmarked skin shone like teenage acne.

"My marble countertop?" she asked the red, plastic counter which glared up at her scornfully with its curling red grin, showing the white underside of its belly.

"What happened to my tall, wide, refrigerator freezer?" she questioned the short, squat icebox that hummed its own curses over the silence of the room.

Her body sagged and she felt at least a dozen years older.

"My view of the vegetable garden?" she whispered mournfully, holding back a tear from an eye that would rather have been closed to the scene. Her energy seeped away from her, and as she looked out the window, the overflowing garbage cans in the alley below didn't answer her either, they just hung their lids in shame.

She closed her eyes and it all went away.

When Lynda and Chad split up, Chad decided he would keep the big screen TV that they had shared, leaving Lynda to take the small one they had in the kitchen that only worked when the weather was calm. He kept the entertainment center with state of the art sound, so that he could wind down from his stressful job. Their two, new, advanced-technology computers were set aside for him because he needed them both for his work, generously leaving Lynda the stumbling, geriatric 18 pound desk computer that took the scenic route when booting up, instead of the highway. All of the artwork remained with him in order to impress visiting clients and all of the furniture, because it had been bought specifically for that house. Oh, and of course the house itself, won in a coin toss with a two-headed dime. In all fairness, because he was a kind and charitable man, he allowed Lynda half of the items they had bought together. And he was unanimous in those decisions.

She opened her eyes and it all came back.

Standing in her new kitchen, Lynda was suffering from downgrade shock. Her state-of-the-art clean kitchen was a mere memory that lingered thin and wispy, like the scent of a roast beef dinner. Suddenly she was on her knees on the splintered wooden floor, weeping with despondency, desperation and despair and then the phone rang. Rising up slowly from the floor, knees decorated with yellow grease spots and black Rorschach Test-shaped morsels from prior tenants, she stumbled to the phone. It was him. Her ex. He was calling to see how she was doing! Happiness and relief ran through her and every one of her problems immediately disappeared, as if released from a magic spell.

"How are you doing?" he asked her. "How's the new place?"

"It's fine," she answered bravely, picking off a lump of black goo from her left knee and staring at it. "I miss you."

"I miss you too," he answered. "Listen, the reason I'm calling is because I'm wondering where the small spoons are. I need to have one for my yogurt and I can't find any."

A big fat silence followed that seemed to find its way into her head and then expand, making his words echo around inside.

She wanted to say to him "you heartless man, why don't you have your girlfriend make a spoon with her thumb and finger and feed you your damn yogurt from her hand," but she didn't. She hung up the phone and looked around at her miserable little kitchen. Then she gazed unblinkingly at the black sticky mess on her finger. It reminded her of him and she smeared it on the wall. "There goes Chad," she said to herself with a satisfied smile on her face. "One day at a time." And every time she looked at the smear of greasy old nothing on the wall, it reminded her of his unkindness and she knew she was going to be all right without him.

Comment

After your relationship ends, you might find yourself like Lynda, downgrading perhaps from townhouse to trailer. Others may have benefited from their breakup, moving from ghetto to grandeur, but whether you are the abandoner or the abandonee, about 50 percent of people wake up in a strange place after a breakup, and it's not always because they drank too much the night before and went home with the bartender. It's hard to adjust to many new things, but to adjust to something unpleasant is worse.

Don't you hate those people who say there is good to be found in everything? It's easy to agree with that if you find it easy to fool yourself, but who wants to call himself a fool? It may be true that something good is on its way, but it's not coming through the dark at you on an express train. It's coming on a local train that makes many stops along the way before it reaches you, and there are plenty more corners for it to turn. There's fog to navigate, rain to ward off and it still has to find its way to the end of the tunnel where they say the light is. So while it takes its own sweet time rumbling along the tracks and slowing down for cattle, pat yourself on the back for getting to step one of your new life. You have to start somewhere and it just isn't easy. But you are still here on this planet and hopefully all of your body parts are functioning and still intact. Yes, that first day might be full of surprises, but like Lynda, you may be reminded very quickly why it was that you and your ex broke up.

Reality Check Versus Dreams
Bring on the ax murderer

*M*agic tricks are great. If we had magical powers, we would grab back that lost love and make them stay with us until we were ready to let them go. So, because our powers are limited, what would we settle for? Another chunk of a week with Serena? A slice of a day with Vinnie? Or a morsel of a moment with the lovely Belinda? Would that be enough to get you through the day, or would it just be the appetizer that wets your palate and makes you cry out for more, more, more?

The Tale of Ginny

Ginny was in the house with Elliot and they were having a snack of some star-shaped purple and green food in front of the television. Ginny was wearing a blue and yellow winter scarf with pink and orange sequins and Elliot had just come back from swimming in the frozen lake and was dripping water all over the couch. Ginny leaned on Elliot as they sat and ate, and she was aware of his body warmth through his shirt. She could feel his regular breathing as it gently rocked her shoulder up and down. There was no conversation but an easy atmosphere made talking unnecessary between lovers. As Ginny noticed a fish sticking out of his pocket she idly wondered if it was a trout or a pike and then she woke up in bed. She had been having these dreams about Elliot since they broke up about three months ago, and when she woke up they felt so real that she would believe for that short window of time that they were still together.

So for a moment she lay in bed with her eyes still closed, feeling content and relaxed because she didn't yet realize it was That Dream again. Her brain began to awaken and she tried to keep it sleeping so that the illusion wouldn't be broken. This time she burrowed deeply into the bed, as if she could hold onto the dream by doing that. Unfortunately, the bouncer of reality was already throwing it into the back alleyway of her thoughts and Elliot's memory was being pummeled away.

The dream of a life with Elliot disappeared as new sleep pushed its way in and another dream came under the spotlight to take its place. As she slept again, she dreamt she was in a cornfield this time and an escaped criminal was chasing after her. It was the typical dream where you run and run and seem to stay in the same place. The corn reached out to her, grabbing her legs and arms and pulling her back like a vegetable octopus. As she looked behind her, the criminal was catching up and the shine on his bald head reflected the sun, momentarily blinding her, and she stumbled to the ground. The convict was wearing an orange, prison-issued jumpsuit with Ginny's mother's telephone number on the front as his inmate number. He looked exactly like Evan Ross, the weatherman from Channel 11 News, who Ginny's mother had a crush on. Evan looked down at her and his gold teeth glinted as he said, "I'm going to kill you, then I'm going to kill all of the small animals on this earth."

"No, no!" Ginny cried, shielding her face with her arms. "Please, at least spare the endangered ones!" A cartoon criminal-type laugh filled the air as he leant forward and beat her with the tassels that cascaded from the top of an ear of corn. As she writhed and dodged the blows she woke herself up. Lying in bed trembling with fear, heart racing and sweat running down her body, she managed a weak smile. "Thank God it wasn't another dream about Elliot," she whispered to herself, with a sigh of satisfaction.

Comment

It's true that you should be careful what you wish for. Your subconscious is always alert and is over-enthusiastically trying to run your life. Unfortunately, it doesn't always have a sense of what's best for you. Ginny wanted her life back with Elliot and the recurring dreams she had about him were so realistic that they allowed her to live in the past for a few snatches of time.

While her dreams played, they were wonderful nightmares, giving her a taste of what she no longer had, but in the haziness of waking up they were ripped away from her like a band aid stripped off by an angry doctor.

Are dreams more real when you are vulnerable? Right after a breakup we worry about everything. Our brain tries to calm us down and organize our thoughts, but these fears come out in dreams. They mix themselves up with something ordinary we see on TV, like an ad for a scarf with pink and orange sequins and somehow that shows up in our dreams. If we are wearing that ugly scarf in public, it's more likely to be nightmare. After a separation, every day is a healing day and we often don't recognize that our body and brain are doing everything they can to help us recover. But as far as wishful thinking goes, a real, cold nightmare can be better than having that slice of a dream about a lost love. Is it worth having just a taste of something we can't have? Where is the ax murderer with the three eyes and the drooling smile? Tell him I'll meet him tonight in my dreams.

Reunited, Giving It Another Try
"And on the seventh day they rested."

I t works for movie stars—marry, divorce, and then marry that same person again. Everyone's heard of someone this applies to. Why shouldn't it work for you?

The Tale of Jasmine and Jerome

Jasmine and Jerome had broken up four weeks ago and every week they were apart seemed like a month to them, and that's how they knew they were still in love. They spoke on the phone and angels could be heard, distantly playing harps on the line between the crackling sounds because their love was so perfect. The gods were smiling down on them and when Jerome suggested Jasmine move back in with him she was delighted.

Their reunion was like the first time they felt their love. It was the honeymoon they always wanted and couldn't afford and now they would be together forever and they knew this time their relationship would work. It was so perfect and their happiness with each other was salad bar never-ending. It was day one.

Another day in the paradise of suburbia; there was an air of contentment all around the house spreading from room to room, like the scent from a fake candle. They felt very comfortable with each other and were extremely polite and respectful. They did things for each other without expecting reciprocity. Jerome bought Jasmine a beautiful bouquet of wildflowers that he said expressed his love for her, "… because her beauty was like a flower." How could they ever have broken up? It was day two.

Another happy day followed. Relief at being together was palpable. The home had an air of relaxation about it, like the end of a vacation, when you've done and seen everything and are just sitting down now to read the newspaper. They gave each other a little space to breathe, but always smiled when they saw each other. The sex was the best. It was the vacation after the vacation. It was day three.

It was a rainy day and her car wouldn't start and there wasn't time for breakfast, but Jerome dropped Jasmine off at work. They kissed each other goodbye and when they said, "I'll miss you," they really meant it, but in a mechanical kind of a way. After work they went out to eat, but it was just fast food and they didn't talk much because that day there wasn't much to say. When they arrived home, they watched television in separate rooms and then went to bed together. The sex was still good, albeit uncreative. It was day four.

Everything went smoothly, the car was fixed, the sun was shining, they were together and they were in love. But somehow it felt as if there was a full moon, because there was a restlessness in them both, which they had never experienced before. They talked more that day than they had ever talked before, but the conversation was polite and guarded, as it would be with a client after too many brandies. But they were together, in love and making this thing work. And that was all that mattered. It was day five.

There was something of an awkward atmosphere in the house; a little like the tension that occurs after an argument with an insurance company. They didn't eat together because Jerome had brought food home for one, and Jasmine had already cooked for herself. Conversation was a little hesitant while they held hands and watched a late, long movie together, so that they wouldn't have to have sex. It was day six.

Jasmine watched him drinking milk directly from the container and Jerome was irritated by her disapproving look. She didn't bother picking up her clothes from the bedroom floor and he realized that she hadn't picked them up all week. At the end of the day, they had a huge argument about a jar of pickles, brought on by irritability with each other. Jasmine packed a bag and went back to her mother's. She didn't look back. Jerome had an early night and watched the game. It was day seven.

Comment

Sometimes getting back together can look like a Hollywood movie set. Everything seems perfect at first glance. The buildings give the impression of being solid and real. The lawns are manicured and the flower gardens are beautiful. Your relationship begins in an ideal manner and everything appears to be strong and permanent. But after a while you start to notice things behind the beautiful façade. Those sturdy looking houses on the movie set have no substance behind them and are merely a thin wooden front held up by support beams in the back. Your relationship might be of the same construction, seemingly strong, but not strong enough to withstand a major thunderstorm or disagreement. Those beautiful-looking flowers on the set are fake. Look closely at them and you will see paint was used to touch up their brightness, and there's some dust clinging to the petals.

Are you painting your love a little too brightly, being just a bit too amorous and abnormally cheerful, only to lose interest again in a few weeks when your façade fades and you become your own cranky self again? The fake garden on a set can be rolled up and put away when the rain comes down. Will you be thinking of leaving when things get tough again?

Think carefully about getting back together. Nothing changes once you are really back into it, and you have to decide if that's what you want. Often, you can compare it to the best vacation you ever had. If you try to go back, it's never as good as the first time; the locals are not as friendly and the drinks are always weaker and sometimes it rains all week. You should stick with the good memories you are left with and call it a day. However, some people realize they want to stay together. They may have missed their ex so much that they are willing to make it work. If you think you are one of those people, know then there is a lot of hard work and commitment ahead of you. After all, King Kong wasn't built in a day.

Keeping Your Partner's Junk
A museum for the soul

Your partner moved out and took the things that they wanted and said, "you can keep whatever else you want. I don't need the rest of this stuff." Could that possibly mean that they might be thinking of coming back to you? Surely if they were going to be gone forever, they would have taken their sea shell collection and broken TV set with them, and not just the new electronics and framed pictures? Is it worth living in hope? Should you tenderly look after their discarded items in case they come back to reclaim them? It doesn't sound like it, but you feel you ought to leave a love candle burning in the window for them anyway.

The Tale of Martin

Martin had always been something of a collector. Others, who were more judgmental would say "more of a hoarder." In his younger days he used to collect baseball cards, autographs and small rocks. He currently collected stamps, beer bottle caps, comic book memorabilia and rubber bands. He had been with his girlfriend Kathy for four years and then she left him for an eminent physician who often appeared on television. When Kathy moved out of the apartment she shared with Martin, she left some of her remnants behind, telling Martin to throw them out.

Being a collector, it seemed natural for Martin to hold on to these items that were left, "just in case she comes back and needs them," he would explain to people when they visited and accidentally sat on a clay figurine of one of the seven dwarfs, or made themselves comfortable with a baby panda cushion. They would nod their heads sadly and do that thing that people do when they purse their lips and look down at their laps. "Poor guy," they would think to themselves, "He can't help himself. It won't be long now until they bring in the straitjacket."

They were savvy to the fact that when your lady leaves you for a cardiologist whose parents own a liquor store and whose brother is a movie producer, she aint never coming back. Sometimes the grass is just a whole lot greener on the other side. But Martin, ever the optimist, held onto Kathy's belongings because they made him feel closer to her. And, he truly believed she would come back to him one day, therefore, he had to be sure that nothing of hers was missing.

Inside the box of items Kathy had discarded was Mr. Biggles, her teddy bear from when she was a child—the one with the dangerous metal spike where its eye used to be, which she used to sleep with before it went partially blind and potentially lethal. Also in the box was a popcorn necklace Martin made for her one drunken Valentine's Day. He was sure she would want to wear it on her return to him, and he kept checking it carefully for signs of insect infestation, as he didn't want it to be eaten by ants or flies. He even kept a shopping list she had written many months ago. Now it was looking somewhat faded because he would sometimes rub it against his face, transferring the DNA of the hand that touched the paper onto his cheek, so that he could savor it:

"b-u-t-t-e-r, p-a-s-t-a, m-i-l-k; important things for her to remember when she came back to him and wanted to cook him a meal.

Martin waited many weeks for Kathy to return to collect her leftover things, but unfortunately that day never came. It took him a month to gather up his emotions so that he could remove Mr. Biggles from his bed and another three days before he stopped using her toothbrush. As for the shopping list, it had already turned into dust, thanks to his beard stubble. Poor Martin had been hoping in vain.

Comment

It's normal to think your ex might call, stop by or even take you back if that's what you are hoping for. Sometimes that happens when people are not hoping for it, and that can be remedied by having a lawyer draft a restraining order, but that's another story and one with a high bill attached to it.

Keeping their things around in case they come back and need them is fine, just put them away in a box in the basement with all of your other memories of them and in time, torrential rain may seep in and destroy everything, so luckily you will never have to decide what to do with them. It's more than a little creepy to keep their discarded things so that you can brush your teeth with their DNA, so once the weeks have passed by and your ex hasn't, it's time for a cleansing of the mind, body and home. Once you feel the relationship has finally come to an end, focusing on the maybes can be a waste of time, and sometimes it can be downright dangerous. Especially if you are sleeping with a teddy bear that has a spiked metal grudge for an eye.

Talking About the Ex
A lesser-known sleep aid

reakup Limbo is the phase where the bruises of the breakup are reflected all over your heart and your mouth just won't stop making comments about how wonderful or terrible your ex was. You will go through the Ex Talk phase. There is no avoiding the Ex Talk phase. It comes right after the Did This Really Happen to Me? phase, and immediately before the Screw My Ex and the Boat They Came In On phase. It will be known among your friends as the Here They Go Again stage or the Lethally Boring era.

The Tale of Dennis

Christine was a very attractive lady, who wore her hair up in a clip because otherwise it frizzed out all over town, and when she wore high heels, she believed they made her look slimmer and waif-like. She broke up with Dennis because she met someone else who she imagined had a little more class than he did, and if that's what someone is looking for, good luck to them. Dennis was a t-shirt and beer kind of man who liked footballs and meatballs. When Christine left him, he was devastated and he put her up on a pedestal, because he still adored her and couldn't get her out of his mind. He lived, breathed and existed only for Chrissie. His friends felt sorry for him and took him out to football games, movies, dinners, in fact, all things to try to help him forget her.

When his friend Colin had a Superbowl party at his house, he invited Dennis. Conversations with Dennis went like this:

Colin: "Dennis, would you like a dark ale?"

Dennis: "Sure, I'll take one. Chrissie was dark, you know. Dark complexion, dark eyes."

Colin: "Yes, I remember. So did you watch the game last night? Who would have thought the Penguins would have won in the last minute?"

Dennis: "No, I don't like hockey, but Chrissie used to like penguins. One time we went to the aquarium and we saw the penguins there. Chrissie bought a purse that looked like a penguin. She kept her loose change in it."

Colin: "Well, that's really interesting. I'm going over to talk to Rich now. I'll catch you later."

Craig: "Hi, Dennis. Come over and get some food."

Dennis: "Thanks, Craig. Chrissie liked food you know. She was such a good cook. She used to make me my favorite food, hamburgers. Hey, Craig, you got any hamburgers over there?"

Craig: "Yes, we've got hamburgers and foot-long hot dogs, too."

Dennis: "Ah, yes. Foot longs. Chrissie's feet were quite long, you know, for a girl of her height. But they didn't look bad because she had nice toes. Did you ever see her toes, Craig?"

Craig: "Can't say that I did, Dennis, but I'm sure she had great toes. I'll just go and get you that hamburger now."

Javier: "Hi, Dennis. How's it going? Did you see the new movie that just came out with that hot Elaine Brown?"

Dennis: "I haven't seen it, but don't you think that Chrissie's hot? She looks a bit like Elaine Brown, don't you think?"

Javier: "Well, er, no, not really. I mean Elaine's half Chrissie's age."

Dennis: "Half? Chrissie used to buy half and half for my coffee. Now I just take regular milk."

Comment

Do you hear what Dennis is saying? Can you hear what you are saying? Are you also talking your friends into a coma about your ex? Once you realize that they have started avoiding you, it might be because you are talking about your ex ad nauseum and not realizing it. The Temporarily Devastated And Hurt don't hear what they are saying. They don't realize they have been reduced to a blobby pathetic mess while they wind their way through the Ex Talk phase. You need to consciously try to monitor what comes out of your mouth, otherwise your friends will be falling asleep all over the place. This, in turn, can be lethal if your friend is driving a car or flying a six-seater aircraft at the time. Ex Talk people should be gently reminded by their friends that enough is enough. If you were ever the recipient of such talk, you'll understand. Besides Ex Talk people, other people to avoid are angry people. Anger is infectious, like watching someone vomit. Pretty soon you'll have to do it, too.

Building a Shrine to Your Ex
Don't live in the ShrineLike Zone

Your partner moved out about five week ago and it was understandably a difficult transition. But your home still looks like they live there. Do you want to see little reminders of them wherever you look? The indentation of a rounded behind on a sofa cushion perhaps can't be helped, but a coffee cup with their lipstick on the rim placed strategically on top of the TV like a trophy? How about stiff little beard trimmings on the side of the sink?

After a while you need to move on and put away the memories of your old love. Or, at least, wash the sink with bleach and run the dishwasher. But what if you can't bring yourself to do that? Then you have probably created the ShrineLike Zone, which is very much like the Twilight Zone in its eeriness. This zone manifests itself in a home that houses one person with a shrine to their ex who moved out some time ago. Because you're not three years old anymore you shouldn't have any imaginary friends, so why are you keeping a home for two people? Creepier and creepier.

The Tale of Molly

Molly retained the marital home after Bob moved out, because Bob knew that she would have a hard time adjusting to a new place after their years together, plus he felt guilty over the breakup. He knew that was the right way to feel and despite leaving her, he always did the right thing. Five weeks after Bob moved out, Molly's old school friend, Kris, came to visit her. Kris had visited Molly on many occasions because she lived nearby, but she hadn't stopped by to see Molly since Bob moved out.

When she entered the house, she was surprised to see that nothing had changed from when Bob lived there. It wasn't just that the furniture was the same, Kris had expected that, it somehow seemed that Bob had only stepped out for a moment, perhaps to buy a newspaper, and then he would be right back. His armchair was empty, obviously not surprising, but it was still situated directly in front of the TV, facing the fire, warming its empty self and making the fabric sleepy. Molly sat in her faded old armchair where the springs made themselves intimately unwelcome and the upholstery poked its elbow rudely into the small of her back. Kris saw her shiver because her chair stood where it always had, off to the side of the fire and the television, giving her a sideways view of the screen and only a breath of heat from the fireplace.

Kris wondered why Molly hadn't moved her chair to a better location, or why she wasn't using Bob's chair. His chair had thick seat padding, soft new cushions, an elevated footrest and luxurious upholstery. Then she realized Molly was being polite by leaving that chair open for her this evening. As Kris gratefully sat down in Bob's warm, comfortable chair, Molly sprang up from her seat and reprimanded Kris, "Please get out of that chair, that's Bob's chair. No one is allowed to sit there! Please go and sit on the couch." Kris stood up and faced Molly.

"But Molly," she reasoned, "Bob's not here anymore. Anyone can sit in that chair, including you." The look on

Molly's face, red with agitation, was enough of a warning to Kris to say no more.

Kris reluctantly left the hospitable chair and made her way to the bathroom. As she passed by the bedroom, she glanced in and stopped for moment because something strange had caught her eye. Making sure Molly didn't see her, she slipped in. There in a corner was a pile of Bob's clothes that looked as though they been thrown down by the owner after wear, presumably headed for the dirty laundry basket. Except these clothes had a low, white, doggie gate in front of them, keeping them safe from harm, or possibly intruders. It reminded Kris of the detective programs on television, where police tape was put around the crime scene to stop people from tampering with the evidence. What on earth was going on, she wondered?

When Kris returned to the living room, she grudgingly sat on the chilly couch next to an overflowing ashtray which held Bob's cigarette butts. She knew they were Bob's because Kris didn't smoke, and she knew that Kris had discouraged all visitors since Bob had moved out. It was an ashy DNA remnant of sadness and tar. Kris saw that the TV was tuned to football, because Bob often watched football even though Molly detested it. Kris was beginning to become spooked by her friend's irrational behavior and as she settled down to watch the Giants play the Dolphins, a small smear of movement caught her eye in the kitchen. She turned her head to look and saw a dull brown shadow reflected on the kitchen counter. It was block-shaped and had a strange type of movement to it, like a flag waving in a halting breeze or a belly dancer waving a soft, chiffon scarf around her body. "That's what it is," thought Kris, "a billowing type of movement—

an uneven soft wave." So there was a riddle: what's brown and billows softly in a kitchen? Kris walked over to investigate and was immediately disgusted at what she saw. It was an army of ants carrying away chunks of pepperoni pizza!

Mesmerized, Kris watched as the brown shadow that was an army of ants, six little bodies across and never-ending in length, came in under the back door, up a chair leg, then onto the counter, all in perfect formation. They entered empty-handed, or rather, empty-mandibled, waited their turn in the pizza line, then left with a delectable, five-week old chunk of mozzarella cheese and dough in their jaws. Yum yum. It was cartoon animation transformed into real life.

"Molly? How long has this pizza box been here?" called out Kris from the kitchen.

"Oh, don't touch that box," responded Molly, extracting herself from an over-friendly seat spring. "I want to keep it. It's what's left of the pizza that Bob ate the night he moved out." She entered the kitchen and saw the ant army, who were unfazed at being discovered by the owner of the house. Her hands covered her face. "Oh my God!" she exclaimed.

And so the ShrineLike Zone began to wind itself down. Arming themselves with their own weapons to fight this formidable army of perhaps thousands, Kris with last Sunday's newspaper and Molly with a can of bug spray, began to remove one of the many shrines to Bob that Molly had created. Pretty soon the miniature army had been wiped away to another dimension, far, far away from the ShrineLike Zone.

Comment

If you find yourself maintaining a shrine after your partner moves out, nip yourself in the bud, or wherever a nip might do you some good. Your life has changed since then and your environment should reflect this change. Make your home your own and put away the things that belonged to your ex. You can take your time adjusting, there's nothing wrong with that, but if you have been living this way for more than five weeks, or if stale food is involved, it might be time to check out of the ShrineLike Zone.

Broken Up or Pity Sex
Getting lucky through guilt

*I*t's natural for people to confuse sex with love, because often in a committed relationship, sex is love and love is sex. It's similar to the three musketeers' motto "All for One and One for All." But if you are outside of a committed relationship, sex is supposed to be fun and love is only found in poetry. As we get older love lives on contentedly without sex, unless one of the oldsters gets themselves a hot boy toy or girl toy, and that's yet another story. A fascinating story, really, but this isn't it.

When love is gone or taken a turn in a different direction and the couple is no more, they may still have a sexual draw to one another. The pheromones are still dancing in the air between them and it takes a big puff of reality to blow them away.

The Tale of Ashley

Three weeks after Mike broke up with Ashley he stopped by to see how she was. When he said, "Hi," and hugged her, an old yearning kicked in. Like aspirins can lead to heroin, hugs can lead to sex and that's what happened. There could be a multitude of reasons why they jumped on each other like rabbits playing leapfrog, and because every relationship has its own idiosyncrasies, it's a waste of time speculating why.

Ashley felt that the intimacy of his hug brought back feelings of love and security, and it was natural for her to want to have sex with him. But Mike loved his new girlfriend, so why did he have sex with Ashley? Maybe for the same reason people climb mountains: because they are there.

But whatever the reason, it became a ritual between them. Every week Mike would say goodbye to Jessica, his girlfriend, and stop by Ashley's home to kindly offer his lovemaking. Following their moments of passion, she would bask in the afterglow alone, while Mike basked in the afterglow in his car on the way home to his girlfriend, at which point the basking and the afterglow would come to a screeching halt.

As the weeks passed by, Ashley's afterglow began to flicker and dim. Once it had fizzled out, the during glow also diminished and the ritual turned into sex, then it became just "a quickie," which satisfied neither of them. When the passion was gone, Ashley knew it was time for the ultimate goodbye and time to nix all of those conjugal visits.

Comment

At the time of the breakup, it took Ashley a while to come to terms with the fact that Mike had left her. She needed more time to let him go. Unlike Ashley, you may not have an ex-partner to considerately give you flesh time, so bear in mind you could be sexless for a while. Sex is what kept Ashley close to Mike when she needed a warm body to hold next to her heart, and he was kind enough to oblige her. What a guy! Perhaps just sleeping in the same bed overnight with him would have given her the same fulfillment, but all women know it's impossible to find a man who would do that. You're half undressed, he's half undressed, he's fully undressed and oops, what's that? But pity sex dies a hard death because it isn't meant to be anything more than an infrequent grope in the dark. You are better off holding out for new-person sex. New is the new "New," you know.

Regret for Past Mistakes
Too sore to sit from kicking ourselves?

What is regret? If we feel we contributed to breaking up a good relationship and we could kick ourselves for doing it, that's regret and guilt is usually just a spit away. Perhaps we feel sorry that we lost our temper when we called our partner's sister a no good, lying, toad-faced witch. We may feel remorse at the revenge we took when we went into our partner's dresser drawer and threw out one sock from each pair, or snipped out the feet from their pantyhose. Did we try the excuse of, "I can't help it," or "You'll have to forgive me, it's just the way I am," too many times? Perhaps we just made one big, fat, terrible decision that can't be forgiven? Or are our indiscretions openly hanging out there for the world to judge, like so many pairs of stained underwear pinned to the clothesline? Maybe we just tried too hard. So was it really our fault and should we still be losing sleep over it months later?

The Tale of Mia

Mia and Brandon began their married life in a one-bedroom house that was ancient and drafty and which noticeably leaned to the right, but not politically. They shared this house not only with each other, but also with little multi-legged garden creatures that came in through the cracks in the walls and through invisible gaps around the door. The ugliest ones came at night to pick at crumbs that were left on the counter and they were brown and crackly and had waving antennae that twitched and probed and relentlessly found food. But nothing much mattered to Mia and Brandon except their love for each other. Mia wanted to make her new husband happy and she cooked and cleaned their little roach-infested love nest and adorned it with cheap knick-knacks from the local dollar store; optimistically installed roach motels; and decorated their three rooms with love and hope.

Equally, Brandon wanted to impress Mia. These days, men don't traditionally need to hunt anymore to bring home The Goods to their partners, but they still feel a need to bring something to the table, if not necessarily freshly-killed deer, rabbits or cold water fish, then money to buy those things either fresh or frozen. Brandon wanted to make Mia happy and have nice things like jewelry, a big house and, of course, fish whenever she wanted it.

To that end, Brandon secured a job with a large corporation in the city and he was determined to work his way to the top. Because he was a bright man, his success was quick in coming and pretty soon they had moved out of their infested abode in the forest into a splendid one bedroom house in the suburbs. In order to pay the mortgage every month, Brandon had to work overtime one night a week. Now Mia no longer had to shop at the dollar store and was finally able to buy name-brand cleaning products. As time went by, Brandon put together a deal that earned him a promotion and they immediately sold their spotlessly clean one bedroom house and moved into a bright two bedroom house that faced south and was sunny all day long. In order to meet the higher mortgage, Brandon now worked two nights a week and although Mia grumbled at seeing him less often, she kept his meals warm in the oven and waited until 10 p.m. two nights a week to dine along with him.

Soon Brandon's firm became more impressed with him and promotions followed one after the other, and each time his pay increased, so did the size of their home. But like any tale that contains a story of life and a little house in the forest, there is a moral. And that's something no one likes to hear. Each time they moved and upgraded their home, Brandon had to work one extra night to keep up with the bills and by the time they were living on the Palatial Estates in Rockefeller City in their seven bedroom house, Brandon was working overtime seven nights a week. Mia rarely saw him and missed him terribly—the money had become of secondary importance to her and she longed for the love they had when they lived with the scavenging insects of the forest in their first home, just off the beaten path from the dollar store.

During the short hours when Brandon was home, he didn't seem to notice Mia anymore. He was continually on the phone and if his ear wasn't flashing the blue light of a call from a client, his cell phone was pressed against his ear. He was distracted by a call one morning at breakfast, and she watched him mistakenly put butter and then jam onto his hash brown, believing it was toast, and then eating it. To her, the saddest part was that he didn't notice the difference. Everyday life as rational people know it had lost its meaning to him and when he was not on the phone, he was planning his next call. He had ceased to live in the present moment and lived only in the cellular future. The dinners that she kept warm for him had now stopped—she was tired of apologizing for re-heated peas that were BB gun pellet hard, and fresh fish that became curled and hard like cheap linoleum. When she asked him to accompany her to social events on the weekend or to help run errands she was no more than his Pied Piper, as he would blindly follow her with his head down, walking wherever she walked and concentrating on his calls, blue light flashing like a police car on its way to a domestic dispute.

And how did Mia feel now that she had her palatial mansion and furnishings from the Million Dollar Store? Lonely, unloved and bored out of her mind. Mia was lonelier in their big house than she had been in the smaller one, because there was more space in which to be lonely. During those long, solitary nights she would walk from room to room, counting the bedrooms as she walked through them. It became a ritual and after a while she would pause in bedroom number five to stare at Floyd Watkins through the bay window as he undressed for his evening shower. Loneliness was making her a voyeur and she hated herself for that. Once she started showering along with him in his house she hated herself even more, but at least she wasn't lonely and it eased the tedium of bedroom counting.

Mia and Brandon's fairytale marriage was now lying on its back, legs akimbo and kicking like an expiring housefly and Brandon hadn't seen this coming, despite constant reminders from Mia. Once the split was official, he regretted putting his career first. He still loved Mia as much as ever and of course he never tired of her because he didn't spend enough time with her to get bored. But his biggest regret was not noticing sooner that Mia had moved out of their seven bedroom home. Four days passed before he realized she had gone and he may not have noticed for a week if he hadn't been climbing into bed one night in the small guest bedroom (bedroom number five), so as not to awake Mia who slept in the master bedroom (bedroom number one), and saw her in the house across the way undressing for her evening shower with their neighbor, Floyd Watkins. Because it had taken him four days to realize that she had gone, he was too humiliated to ask her to come back to him. He also didn't want to antagonize Floyd—a much bigger man than he in every way. So Brandon lost the woman he loved and he was to blame, and he hated himself for it. The regret lingered on for years. Sometimes something has to be gone before you realize it used to be there. But it's even more disturbing if you can't remember what the heck it was.

Comment

When we look back at our past behavior we may wonder, "What *were* we thinking?" At the time we believed we were doing the right thing, but in retrospect our actions seemed like those of a reckless incompetent. But self-blame lingers on like a winter's ache in the bones and reminds us of past weaknesses. But lingering on our past mistakes is only a form of self torture and who wants to be tormented when we are at our most vulnerable?

It's a strange peculiarity of human nature, but if something goes wrong and it's not our fault, we somehow find a way to blame ourselves anyway—sometimes partially and sometimes entirely. It's possible that Mia felt she contributed to the failed marriage over the years and even now still harbors regret, when in fact she did all that she could do to hold the relationship together until it was washed away down the shower drain.

So forgive yourself for those bad things you did or thought you did, and for the mistakes you made, because everyone has at least one huge regret. If we hadn't done those specific regretful things, we would have done others. That's what being human is all about and we are not perfect. So take some mouthwash and flush out the regrets, spit out the remorse and say, "Aaah. A lesson learned and I am a better person for it." As for the guilt, it's just you giving yourself a hard time, and that's something best left for your mother to do.

First Day Alone
When what you didn't do, is all you did

So, you have survived the first hour of your day and the rest of the non-working day is dragging by like a war-wounded centipede with 50 legs missing. The first day after a separation is the most difficult one because you may be in shock or denial and of course, everything is new and the future is terrifying. You must bite the proverbial bullet and face the day the same way the matador faces the bull, head on and waving a red flag.

The Tale of Samantha

Samantha was a pensive woman and economical with her words. When George and Sam broke up, she preferred to struggle through her first day alone, so that she could come to terms with her thoughts and not worry about making conversation with helpful family members. It was a non-day where nothing happened, and that was the most remarkable thing about it. She wandered numbly from room to room like a lab rat inside a maze that gets you nowhere. It got her nowhere. When she tired of doing that, she sat on the floor and stared at the phone for about an hour, using possible psychic powers to make it ring, and for it to be George. It didn't ring.

Another couple of hours were spent wondering where George might be and deciding whether or not to call him. But, finally, she didn't. She then pretended George would be finishing what he was doing so that he could be home with her in an hour. Of course he wasn't, but that deception made for the happiest hour of her day. She sat on a chair looking out the window and watched the daylight until it went away. Then she watched the night for a while, and it didn't go away. Following that, she made some dinner for herself, which she didn't eat. Before bed, she sat in front of the television for a while with her favorite show switched on. Which she didn't watch. Lastly, she switched off the waking world and went to bed. She didn't sleep.

Comment

You see? It's not really a day, it's a mere passing of time to get you through to tomorrow when a healing process can begin and a day is a real day. Sam did everything that was expected of her those first 24 hours alone where nothing was on the menu. She walked past events that were waiting to happen, giving them no encouragement so that in the end they went away and primed themselves for a return tomorrow when she would be more receptive. The non-events rattled with the sound of air in a heavy barrel; the sound of nothingness. But once you are safely through those initial hours, you should feel like a war hero and award yourself a metaphorical medal, because the only difference between you and them is the lack of combat.

That first day alone is a toughie. Just watch out for a cloud of smoke following you around. It will be a spectrum of your emotions exploding: anger, tears, despondency, fear, disbelief, so you don't need to wonder why you look like you are smoldering. If this first day without your ex makes you happy instead of sad, you are either having a delayed reaction or you are a very fast healer. Or you are happy just to get rid of that bastard, what's their name?

Crying
Harder to control than a cat that thinks it's in the wrong room

A great big bear cry radiates outward from the heart and initially moves down into the belly where it gains strength and momentum. Then it billows upward through the insides where it spreads outward like molten lava and fills the body with heat, and then a stifled roar emanates from the mouth. That's not only a powerful description, but also one hell of a sad cry and just about the saddest cry that comes from a human being. Sometimes after a split from your lover, the bear cry just comes out. Sadness doesn't get much deeper than that.

The Tale of Carrie

Carrie was born to be afraid of too many things and she was reduced to tears more often than most people. When she was younger, men with muscles made her nervous. Insects gave her the creeps and brought her to tears. Anyone with tattoos made her shake with fear and new situations made her break down and cry. She had always been a crier and she cried her way through kindergarten, especially on the day that Timmy Marshall pushed her into the dirt and muddied up her new yellow sweater with the silver thread. High school was something of a crying era, but as her hormones adjusted, so did her crying. As she matured into a well-adjusted adult, the crying abated.

Her career took off and she started becoming successful and wealthy. In fact, she became so wealthy that she could afford to pay people to cry for her if she wanted. In her late twenties, her crying lessened because that's when she met Gavin. Her marriage to Gavin made her life complete and her tears totally evaporated. Unfortunately, due to a mis-conception (Gavin's mistress accidently conceived), her 10 year marriage ended and the crying began again.

She cried when she woke up and she stopped crying in the shower because there was nowhere to blow her nose. She sniffled while she dressed but took a break while she ate her breakfast. She whimpered as she drove to work and held back the tears until 5:00 p.m. At the end of the workday the waterfall of salty tears flowed strongly and she cried all the way home. "Waaaaaaa." Once she reached home, she blew her nose in the car, dotted her face with a soggy tissue and went into the house. She blubbered while she made herself a tuna sandwich and once she sat down and started eating, the tears took a back seat.

After dinner, she cried herself all the way to the supermarket and sniffled down the frozen food section. Buying ice cream momentarily dried the tears faster than a supersonic hair dryer and she only dripped a little from the nose as she drove home. Twenty minutes after arriving back at home, all of the ice cream was gone and then sniffle led to sob and the howling resumed. That night the neighbors congregated down the hill from her home and began to talk in hushed tones about the movie "Psycho," as strange and eerie howling sounds emanated from the house atop the hill. Perhaps someone was being murdered up there, or was it the sound of a large beast howling? No one dare go up to check.

Saturday followed the work-week and Carrie woke up that morning, stared at her ceiling from the bed and the crying resumed. As she dressed, she bawled and again took a little break while she ate her eggs and toast. She wailed while washing the dishes as thoughts of Gavin ran rampant in her mind. Laundry was assembled and crying accompanied it, but by the time it reached the dryer there was nothing but a whine. She tried to cry harder but all that came out was an exhausted moan that sounded like the wind blowing down a chimney. The next day there was no crying at all because everything had been cried out of her. In fact, she had to drink extra fluids to replace the tears. A couple of days later she forgot to cry. She still remembered how sad she was, but she kept herself occupied and the tears never came back again for Gavin.

Comment

Crying lies deep inside our hurting emotions and if we try not to think about it, it can stay in hiding until it's summoned. Every time we think a sad thought, we peel off a layer of sadness to the next sad thought, and after peeling off so many sad thoughts, we reach the crying layer. It's rather like peeling off the layers of an onion, which can also make us cry. It's a pity there isn't a vegetable that makes us laugh when we peel it.

It's healthy to let your emotions out and then the sad ones can go their own way and not bother you again. Loss is the prime time for crying and it's often something you cannot control, just like a laugh. Sometimes you cry before you think about how sad you are, but that's just your brain being a smartass by beating you to it.

Emotional Baggage

Adding another notch to the neurosis belt
How relationships leave you with emotional baggage

A bad relationship or a bullying partner can make you unsure of yourself. Once these insecurities given to you by your ex begin to stick, they start thinking they are very important and develop delusions of grandeur. They give themselves a title, rather like a king or a queen, but instead of being called King or Queen Doubts-About-Myself, they have a simpler name: Breakup Baggage.

So now your ex has made you vulnerable and your self-doubts begin to grow wildly. What happens next? Here comes a bus to take away your chance of being loved again. Your confidence takes the back seat, maybe never to return. Wave it goodbye. But wait, what's that getting off the bus and coming toward you? It's your overwhelming problems that seemed so small yesterday and look who's coming with them? It's the Regrets family, carrying a big suitcase in each hand; the unlovable twins, Dora and Ike; Cousin Loneliness, and finally, the Insanity Sisters.

Breakup baggage attaches itself to you like a parasite and will live on you forever unless you either embrace and defend it, or throw it under that bus. You can't feel negative about it, because that's what makes it baggage. The first step is to recognize what it is and the second step is to find out if you are carrying it. Your baggage, if recognized by other people, can affect the relationship you are hoping to have with them and you can only shove it under the seat for a while before it begins to show itself in public.

Problem Baggage

Out of the many different kinds of baggage, problem baggage is the easiest one to leave behind, because it didn't exist when you met your partner and hey! You can return it to them when you leave!

Here is a prime example of someone dishing out problem baggage. Lee senses that Mei is thinking of breaking up with him. He panics. He has to act swiftly and cruelly to keep her. (Yes, that's the way to do it!) So he tells her:

"If you leave me, no one else will want you with all of your problems." This comment plants the seed in Mei's mind that she has all kinds of problems other people don't want to deal with, but if she stays with Lee, he would be accepting of them. It's possible she has no problems at all, he's just making her think she does. And if she really does, it's likely she inherited them from Lee anyway.

He's giving Mei "Problem Baggage." Be realistic, Mei, once you are away from him your "problems" will disappear. It's like a simple magic trick. You just need to know where to hide the rabbit.

Mirror-Image Baggage

Now open the door to the Regrets family!

Derek longs for a peaceful life, but Stacy's temperament is like a rocket that's halfway through a countdown, with jet fuel burning and her tanks pressurized, ready to detonate if not handled correctly. When he tells her he is leaving her, Stacy explodes, with fiery angry word fuel all over the place and says, "If you walk away from me right now, you will regret this for the rest of your life." Stacy is handing out "Mirror-Image Baggage," where everything looks normal, but is really backward, like the reflection in a mirror. Derek isn't the one who will have regrets for the rest of his life, Stacy will, but she's making it seem that he will be the loser. Dude, it's all about her: Her regrets, her losses. She is trying to confuse then manipulate him by giving him her baggage, her fears. She is filling his head with her own doubts and if he agrees with what she says, he has just borrowed her fears and added them to his, so now he is carrying Stacy's baggage too, in the guise of his own. Here's some good advice for Derek: return Stacy's baggage to the closet in front of the mirror and just take your own small suitcase on this one-way trip.

Unlovable Baggage

Let's all greet the Unlovable twins, Dora (Unadorable) and Ike (Unlikeable).

Antonio is a hard working man who can't do enough for his girlfriend, Sarah, but she is never able to trust him because he lies about everything. He even lies about small, insignificant things that don't matter, like "I finished the crossword puzzle in red pen," when in fact he finished it in black pen. Sarah has had enough of Antonio and his compulsive lying and decides to leave him. He responds with, "If you leave me, no one will ever love you the way that I do." Antonio is telling Sarah that there could be more loves in her life, but his love is the best love of all. This could be true or this could be a lie. Knowing Antonio like Sarah does, she thinks it's a lie, but he is convincing and she is on the cusp of believing him. Maybe Sarah won't find another love as good, but she might not win the lottery either. There's a whole new world out there for her and often different love is better love.

Loneliness Baggage

Let's give a warm welcome to Cousin Loneliness, carrying his big box of tissues!

Doreen had never lived alone before and was terrified when Wayne said he wanted to move out of their two-room apartment. Their relationship was always close, and not just because it had to be in such a small space, but because they spent a great deal of time together. Doreen thought she could threaten him into staying with her by saying, "One day, when you're all alone with no chance of meeting anyone else, you'll realize I was the best thing that ever happened to you." She may have said that she was the best thing that ever happened to him, but in truth she was only the most recent. She was also threatening Wayne with loneliness baggage by telling him that he will be all alone, and that the very best thing he once had will soon be gone.

The threat of loneliness baggage is just plain blackmail; if you don't stay you can't have companionship in the future. Who does Doreen think she is, Madame Zara with her crystal ball? How does she know what his future holds? Consider this, if Wayne means so much to her now, there's a good chance that someone else will also appreciate him, therefore he may never be lonely again. So until she can prove her crystal ball really works, that threat is not worth looking into, not now and not in the future either.

Insane Baggage

Introducing—The Insanity Sisters!

Kattania is bored with Ron and decides to move out because she has a crush on Jordan. As she is packing her bags to leave, Ron confronts her with this psychological threat: "Why are you leaving? There must be something wrong with you. You can't be normal." Ron is trying to give her "Insane Baggage." The psychology behind this threat is that if she leaves him, she is crazy, but if she stays, she is normal. He is giving her the label of insanity in the hope that the shoe fits. Kattania, don't be tempted. Drop that shoe. Don't even try it on, even though it has one of those cute little bows on the front. Hold it up and make believe you're going to throw it at him. Maybe it would knock some sense into him. Look him in the eye and say, "I am only temporarily abnormal, because you have made me this way. Once I leave you, I will be normal again. You, on the other hand, will always be crazy." In saying this, she is handing his crazy baggage back to him; but it's unlikely that he would want to take it either.

Comment

These sentences are quotes from the book *The Angry Ex's Guide to Guilt and Persuasion*, which doesn't really exist, but should. There are indeed desperate and manipulative people out there who use threats to get what they want from their relationships, especially when they see their partner slipping though their fingers. It's very common to hear these phrases and it's most important you don't believe them. You are caught off-guard when someone tries to fill your head with baggage and your animal instincts of survival will cause you to defend yourself. Your reactions will be heartfelt and powerful; defensive and wounded. You could do any or all of the following, in any sequence:

Swear loudly.

That's often a reaction if the challenging baggage phrase is spoken loudly. Hopefully you know some choice long words to use, but it won't really get you anywhere because a swearing contest is just a swearing contest. There are no prizes and no referees to tell you who came in first and who came in second.

Resort to Violence.

You know you shouldn't. Your mother wouldn't be proud of you.

Cry.

This just makes them think that they are right. If the tears are accompanied by an apology from you, this signifies acceptance of the baggage, and just like excess baggage, it will cost you more in the long run. If you must cry, still refuse the baggage.

Reason.

"Me, lonely? I have money. I can buy friends."

"I won't find love? There's love on every corner in this town."

"Normal? You wouldn't recognize normal if it came in a medicine bottle with a printed label."

Good solid responses. But because this kind of attack comes suddenly, like being poked with an electric cattle prod, you will probably be vulnerable at the time and may accept your share of the baggage. But how do you release it to the skies? It's not something you can put a tag on and check to Marrakesh. It takes longer to get rid of than that. The first step is reminding yourself that this baggage was given to you as a lie and a threat, and now that you are free of the controlling person, you can start releasing the baggage they gave you. Picture the baggage carousel at the airport, where you would only take your own suitcase and leave everyone else's behind. It's just like that, only it doesn't make you dizzy if you stare at it too long.

PART THREE

COMING TO TERMS WITH THE BREAKUP

A Spritzer of Memories, Coping and Thievery

Everyone Is Better Off Than Me
Illusions are better than the dirty truth

We may have the perception that people who are familiar to us by sight, but whom we haven't actually met yet, are better off than us. Our lives are so miserable after the big breakup that we know for sure no one could be feeling as badly as we do. We have cried, contemplated death by junk food, feel we will never ever be happy again, and we have churned out hate and depression. Our aura is splattered with apathy. Our faces are blotchy. Our friends are avoiding us. No one has a sadder life than we do, and no one knows how bad we feel or how unlucky we are. Also, we are resentful of the happy people around us who don't know how much we are suffering. We are at an all-time low and everyone around us seems better off than we are. And we resent them for it.

The Tale of Harry

Harry was the most popular guy on the 5:39 p.m. train from Chicago to the suburbs. He was a burly, affable man with the inflated face of a cherub; with red cheeks, brown curly hair gelled to the style of the month, and a smile more contagious than a midnight yawn. His suits were plentiful and well-crafted and his power ties were soft, silky and confident. He knew everyone on the train, it seemed, and everyone liked him and would vie for his attention. "Hey Harry, how's it going? Come and sit with me, Bud." He was never lacking for an invitation to sit with one of the guys or have a beer with them, concealed in a brown paper bag.

He generally boarded the train with a different female admirer or power groupie each evening and sat with them only for a teasing number of minutes before he was enticed away by a game of cards with the guys, or a can of beer from a friend. He had worked for the same internet company for 10 years, loved his job and made good money. His success, it seemed, had no limits.

Harry was a lucky fella who had a pretty wife who stayed at home with their three perfect children who played sports and excelled at school. He entertained friends and neighbors at his home with pool parties in the summer and sledding parties with aged brandy in the cold months. If you didn't want to be friends with this guy, you wanted to be this guy. Or his wife. Or even his mother. His exuberance for life was contagious and after spending even a few minutes around him you felt energized because you had shared his aura.

While riding the 5:39 one evening, Eric, a long-time commuting companion of Harry's asked Dave G. of Marginal Financial, "Where's Harry these days?" Dave looked furtively around him and moved into the seat next to Eric.

"Didn't you hear?" he whispered conspiratorially, "He's in the loony bin up on the hill." Eric choked on his bagged beer.

"You are kidding me," he coughed. "I don't believe it! He was such a great guy with a perfect life. What happened?"

Harry once did have it all, but no more. His drinking had escalated to above normal proportions and his wife had already exiled him to the basement, well before he lost his job at Sinternet Internet. To his friends on the train Harry seemed the same, but in secret, his world was falling apart. His drinking on the job and declining sales figures caused him to be fired, but the appearance of going to work continued, and everyone around him, including his wife, believed he went to work each day, when in fact, he had a meaningless commute. On the bright side, he achieved an insightful education into the arts, spending each day at museums and galleries in the city and attending *Shakespeare in the Park* plays at lunchtime.

It wasn't until the household checks came bouncing home that he told his wife he had lost his job. She was unforgiving and moved the children and herself to a cousin's house, following a drunken outburst by their father on Memorial Day at their lake house. He threatened to take all of his wife's clothes down to the water's edge and "throw them to the fishes." Yes, Harry seemed the stereotypical man of perfect happiness, the man who had it all. But seeming aint always being.

Comment

In this world of ours, people's lives are often as bland and problematic as our own. The smiling faces of couples looking happy and holding hands are sometimes a front for an unhealthy or stormy relationship, or they might just be having a short smiling break in-between the tears of abject depression. If you get to know these people you will often find yourself to be more fortunate than they are. Some have bad relationships; others have poorly paid jobs; and the man in the designer suit may have sold his wife to slave traders to buy the suit, in order to get the job that in turn will support his five, motherless children. You just don't know, but one thing you do know, rich or poor, employed or not, lonely or lucky, everyone has their share of problems. They just don't wear them on the outside.

So when you think everyone is better off than you are, just remember, appearances can be deceiving. You can't judge a book by its cover. Things are not always as they seem. The grass is always greener on the other side of the fence. You see, this misconception is so common, that countless sayings have been thought up to describe it! So kick off your pity-me shoes and put on your, "I'm better off than you are" smile, and get to deceiving all of those people out there yourself!

Living in the Past
Don't bother looking back, the past is still behind you

It's a different world looking into the rear view mirror of a car, because you are looking at something you have left behind. The view shows only what you have passed by. Life is also like that. If you try to recapture what you had in the past, you may find that things will never be as good again. What was yours back then may have already disappeared around a corner, or at least molded now with age. You may see a car wreck behind you which could be your marriage. It's unsafe to live your life looking behind you, as looking forward through the windshield is the future. Here is a cautionary tale of Tom, a safe and docile driver, but one who lived in the past.

The Tale of Tom

Tom used to be a good driver—cautious, wary and generally alert when passing other vehicles, sometimes even using his blinkers a little too often, although he himself scoffed at such a thing. Since his breakup with Gina, his driving had become careless because she constantly dominated his thoughts when he was driving in his car. Their relationship had been idyllic and their marriage had lasted for 14 perfect years, but Tom was unable to come to terms with the separation. He lived, ate, breathed and loved in the past. The present had no future for him and his future relied on the past. Unfortunately, he also drove his grey, four-door sedan in the past, his eyes gazing often and remorsefully into the rear-view mirror instead of at the road ahead. Hypnotized by thoughts of his lost love, he imagined he saw Gina, sitting quietly for a change in the back seat of his car. She always wore the same black blouse with the top two buttons undone and her legs were always seductively crossed at the ankle. And she stared at him through the rear view mirror of his mind.

On the day that would have been their 15th wedding anniversary, on an already stifling Monday morning in June, he was so preoccupied with looking into the past that he was momentarily oblivious to the traffic ahead. He somehow failed to notice a very large, well-maintained black pick-up truck directly in front of him that had suddenly stopped. Bammmm. His jaw vibrated as cheap grey paint hit the military over-polished chrome of the truck's bumper and made a visible dent. His heart stopped and his fear stood out like a five o'clock shadow. It wasn't the impact alone that caused Tom's head to jerk back and forth like a dashboard hula dancer from a Hawaiian five-dollar store, but the offensive bumper sticker that decorated the highly polished chrome bumper. He read the words.

As his life flashed before him, fear shook him by the shoulders and slapped him in the face a little bit to get him ready for whatever might come next. The words that were at eye level on the bumper sticker went round and round in his head. "Badass M. F., Badass M. F.," only on the bumper sticker the words were spelled out in full...

Tom was a small man, kindly, and some might say nervous, but he opened the door of his little grey car and imagined that he caught a glimpse of Gina also getting out of the car. He straightened his shirt bravely as he approached the giant who was clumping toward him, wanting to look his best before he met his maker. It wasn't too bad. It was only one blow to the stomach and by the time he straightened his body back up to homo sapien again, the giant was gone. Tom looked around him. Where was Gina? He climbed back into his car and looked into the rear view mirror. The backseat of his mind was empty. Gina had finally left. A punishing blow to the gut had cured his rear view mirror syndrome faster than a shot of adrenalin to a main line, and he never looked back again.

Comment

Don't be like Tom and live in the past. Look toward your future. It may be grim now, but the uneven road ahead could have fewer hazards than the relationship you just got out of. Short and sweet says it all.

Bad Memories
The best times of our lives!

*A*fter the big breakup, we may miss our ex so much that past times with those we loved—Big Tessie or Acned Arnold seemed good in retrospect, even though they used to beat us every Friday, ignore us every Monday and throw food at us on holidays. We mistakenly believe times spent with them had to have been good. If we think about how depressing things used to be, we might get into a funk, which in turn would make us jaded and maybe too sad to love again. If we are too sad to love, we would be too sad to reproduce and then people would become extinct. It's our self-preservation that makes us believe certain bad memories were good, and it keeps us wanting to live and breed.

During our relationships we build memories and put the bad ones in a rarely-used corner of our mind where least-remembered thoughts live. When we reach back for those memories, we don't poke around in that forgotten area looking for unpleasant stuff, we look for the good and we find it in the front. This is called selective remembering.

Occasionally we accidentally wander into the dark place where the bad memories lurk together, talking among themselves about how terrible life used to be. We take these bad guys and we draw them out and we either find some good in them, or mistakenly believe them to be entirely good. "Oh, he wasn't really that bad," we say to ourselves. Or, "That embarrassing moment hardly affected me at all."

Looking back, can you remember exactly how the pain of your most intense toothache felt? Or any pain? It's like trying to explain what a boiled potato tastes like, it just can't be done. You know it was bad at the time (the toothache, not the potato, but that depends on who cooked it), but we cannot reproduce that feeling of pain. So when the mind plays the trick of causing you to remember bad times as good ones, you are building memories of illusion.

The Tale of Danny

After Danny and Ella broke up, Danny really missed their mealtimes together. Now that he was alone and had no one to cook for, he felt his life wasn't worth living. But Danny had forgotten how Ella used to deride his cooking. She would mock his macaroni, ridicule his roast beef and criticize his croutons. He was, in fact, a terrible cook, but making meals for Ella was the way he expressed his love for her. She, on the other hand preferred the more conventional way of showing love, by holding hands, kissing and having sex. Ella loved eating food as much as men loved sports, but she had the tolerance of a gay prima donna if the food wasn't cooked to perfection. Mealtimes were fight times between them and they fought like a dog without hormones and a cat with too many. Often, the food would end up flung onto the walls and very often, it would stick.

Sitting at his kitchen table with happy memories of Ella stewing in his mind like cheap steak warming up in a slow cooker, he recalled the time he made sausages for her but didn't notice that each one was individually encased in plastic inside the wrapper. He had unknowingly cooked the whole ensemble in a hot skillet. It wasn't until Ella started pulling melted plastic off her teeth that he realized what had happened. "What are you trying to do?" she screamed at him. "Kill me? I'm eating PLASTIC!" Needless to say, the sausages ended up sticking very well to the walls, almost as well as they stuck to their teeth. Danny looked back with warmth as he remembered how they had laughed about that. "What? Are you crazy?" asked Ella when he next spoke with her. "We never laughed about that, and I wouldn't eat anything you cooked for me for almost three months. In fact, you know I hated your cooking."

Danny didn't believe her and instead of remembering how she used to patronize his pasta, he preferred to recall that she glorified his goulash and honored his omelets. It really wasn't true that any of those mealtimes with Ella were good, but Danny recalled that they were. He needed good memories to keep him company as he sautéed his salmon and heated his jalapenos, and he truly believed she had always enjoyed his cooking. Was there any harm in thinking so? As long as he had no other delusions, it's probably safe to say that being cheerful about something is better than marinating in your own juices.

Comment

Sometimes we know we are fooling ourselves when we turn bad memories into good, but somehow this satisfies a fundamental need. We need to believe what we had back then was good, otherwise our precious time was wasted. We also compare it to how miserable we feel now, when we are alone, and yes, those bad times with your lover may seem a hundred times better than the very best day in present time, because back then you were together. Danny could have called his pal Al Dente who would have told him Ella didn't need him or his cooking anymore and that they really did argue all the time. But he didn't want to believe it.

Memory-turning is one of the few misdirected instincts we have, because it doesn't make much sense, except to an analyst. So when you're feeling warm and fuzzy as you look at the photograph of last year's holiday party, remember, everyone may seem like they are smiling at the camera, when in fact they are all just saying "cheese." So put on your own cheese face, tell your mind to stop fooling you and write down five good memories. I bet at least one of them was bad, but you just forgot that it was.

Anger
Like a loaded gun, it needs to be pointed in the right direction

They say the five stages of grief are denial, anger, bargaining, depression and acceptance. The five phases of being dumped are: lying; crying; murderous rage; alcohol-induced sleep; and finally, the "You Weren't Good Enough For Me, Anyway," phase. The first phase, lying, is when you try to keep the relationship together by any and all means, and lying, unfortunately, is part of what comes naturally. The crying phase is self-explanatory and many go through this stage, but occasionally, some don't, and those people move right along to the "Murderous Rage" phase. This phase is also known as the "Dr. Jekyll and Mr. Hyde," phase, and you, brothers and sisters, are going to be going through it for a little while. You will find yourselves unsociable and angry for no reason at all. Happy one minute and darker than a toe with frostbite the next. You will have moods that can't be found in textbooks and you will never know which mood comes next.

In this frame of mind, everyday tasks in life become neglected and you may stop taking care of yourself and wave the shower goodbye. Your self-destructive behavior may stretch to the Russian roulette of eating expired foods, where consuming something that is three months old is as good as pulling the trigger and seeing if the e-coli bullet has spun into the chamber yet. Luckily at this point, you are only damaging yourself, unless you have invited friends round for dinner (or your ex!), but if it affects the safety of others, it's time to sit down and have a talk with yourself.

Because rage can result in you behaving like an over-testosteroned teenager, you may be irrational and do things you might regret. Your annoyance has reached the point of irritation on a level with a hung-over utilities worker assigned pneumatic drill duty. Your whole body has a headache and everything gets on your nerves. Your eating habits might be affected because you want to punish your body. Comfort in gobbling up masses of sugar may distract you while you are eating it, but minutes later it's rage on! After a time you may not recognize yourself and ask your alter-ego, "Where is that kindly person I used to be?" You imagine yourself transforming from human to werewolf and you can almost hear the crack of your bones as your entire body gets bigger with rage.

So when you find yourself smiling through clenched teeth, that's rage trying to slide out of your mouth at someone. When you hate everyone including your dog and have taken to carrying a big stick, that's anger. When you even hate your favorite pie and throw a slice against the wall, that's not pie-hate. That's bald, unadulterated fury. So be reminded that this is not a good thing, but it will pass. But right before that happens is where the problems start.

The Tale of Faith

Faith had always been a little moody. A common remark of her mother's as Faith was growing up was, "Faith! Don't slam the…" SLAM. "Door." As she grew from teen to adult she was able to control her mood swings a little better, but her anger was still just rage dressed up in a longer skirt. When she and Nate broke up she was not only angry, she wanted to take her anger out on everyone. The thought of Nate made her want to do things they throw people into big city jail cells for, which will not be mentioned here in case it sounds too appealing to an angry person. Her personality was changing and she noticed that her self-control was at an all-time low. She was no longer cautious about her safety, as if her self-preservation was away on sick leave. Consideration for others was all but forgotten, as was her prior respect for small animals and tolerance for old people.

When her friends called her up she was abrupt and wouldn't speak more than a sentence to them. Her sister Cindy cut her telephone ear on the sharpness of Faith's tongue when Faith shouted into the phone, "You don't understand what I'm going through." But Cindy did, and that's why she called. When old, grey-haired Mrs. Bennington with the shuffle-walk from next door called out, "Good morning, Faith!" Faith snapped back, "Morning it is. Good, it isn't," and she spat out her gum onto Mrs. Bennington's prize-winning yellow roses and then trampled her begonias.

On her way to work, she made her customary stop at the donut shop drive-through for coffee. While waiting for her change, she took a sip. "Ick!" The coffee was too milky and she chastised the man at the drive-through. "Is this coffee or is this baby formula?" she growled, waving the spilling drink through the open window at the cowering man. "If you can't even make a cup of coffee, you should stick to mopping floors!" But she drank it anyway and despite its milkiness it somehow made her angrier, and like an unwatched pan on the stove, she was boiling over by the time she arrived at her job.

Stomping angrily over to her desk, she glanced at a newspaper that was lying on Jerry's desk and read the headline *Angry Cab Driver Strangles Snake*, and the onomatopoeia of the word *angry* invited her to be even angrier.

As the day progressed, she noticed people were afraid to look her in the eye because she had the persona of a wild dog looking for a fight with a rival pack. Her once-gentle eyes now challenged everyone, "What the hell are you looking at??!!" She hated everyone and it showed, and the anger drove her into working twice as hard. At 1 p.m. she didn't stop for lunch because she was too enraged to eat, and because she had gained so much momentum from working so hard that she was unable to stop. Toward the end of the day the anger had been worked off and calmness settled in. Unfortunately, at 4 p.m. her bank called about the loan she had taken out with Nate a year ago and the rage simmered up again and spilled all over her desk, and she didn't care who saw it. When the loan officer told her to "have a nice day," she told him where to put his nice day and it wasn't anywhere nice.

By five o'clock she was too angry to say goodbye to her boss, and she left the office without a word to anyone and headed for the parking lot. Her monthly parking ticket was nowhere to be found and the kindly attendant wasn't so kindly anymore when she refused to pay. She reminded him that she parked there every day but it didn't make a difference. Flinging the money out the window at him, she drove off in a dust cloud of uncaring. Her frustration made her angry, then brought her to tears, and then it brought her away from tears again.

When she arrived home she found her weekly parking ticket inside her makeup bag, and in a temper-tantrum she flung her purse against the wall, where it took some time out on the way over to break a lamp. Cursing at the television after eating a bargain pack of candy bars, the evening continued to decline and she discovered there was another level below the anger she felt, and she was sitting in it. Bedtime came and sleep didn't, so instead, a midnight run was made to the fried chicken place. While eating the deep fried thighs, wings and amoeba shapes, she downed a couple of vodka tonics. She was moving into the alcohol-induced sleep phase.

The following day's consequences of anger were as follows:

A bellyache and a hangover.

Weight gain.

Neither her sister nor her friends would answer their phones to her.

Mrs. Bennington from next door purposely sprayed her with the hose while she watered her garden, and she had to go back inside and change. Twice.

The donut place stopped sugaring her coffee then pretended they didn't understand English.

People at work gave her the cold shoulder.

The bank didn't call again, but instead sent threatening certified letters from their attorneys.

The parking lot attendant told her to park elsewhere for calling him a "fatherless freak."

She bought a new lamp on the way home and it wasn't on sale.

But on the bright side, her boss let her leave work early because she had finished all of her work the day before in record time. Faith knew she had to do something to calm the dragon of rage that threw its flames into her blood. She still hated everyone and now she had consequences, because she had made everyone hate her, so then she hated them even more. Hate breeds hate, and she couldn't control it.

When anger feels like an overpowering amount of energy, getting rid of that energy makes the anger melt away. She started playing loud punk music and rap in her car, and when she sang along to the swearing, it made her feel better, and somehow it calmed her. Kickboxing classes were energizing and the relaxed feeling that followed replaced the rage. In the evenings she walked, and then she ran until she was over-exhausted, especially in the rain; she wanted to punish herself because that seemed to quell the fury. Looking for something

to do on a regular basis, she started watching old TV series'
reruns that distracted her for an hour or so each day.

She read books about adventures and ship wrecks that
took her mind away from herself. She 86'ed the caffeine,
and the sugar and fast food were minimized because they
were anger-friendly, and pretty soon she was her normal self
again. Her friends and sister began returning her calls. It's
easy when you know how, and yes, you are allowed to gloat.
She was now ready to move into the "You Weren't Good
Enough For Me, Anyway," phase.

Comment

The overload of energy is easily misdirected. It spills out
from your pores like sweat after a sauna, eventually turning
back into anger again, and it destroy things around you. It
needs to be channeled out otherwise you get an overload,
then a pop and then a spark, much like the reaction from putting in a battery the wrong way around. Run until your legs
feel like lead. It doesn't matter if it's a mile or only ten yards,
it needs to tire you out without giving you a heart attack.
Clean your house or your car. Watch six straight hours of
bad TV. Stroll around downtown or around the mall. Walk
until you can't find your way home. Dance in your living
room until you get a leg cramp. Sing along loudly to music
in your car until you find someone giving you the one-fin-
gered driver's salute. Exercise at the gym until you look like
you're on steroids, but get rid of the energy-to-anger danger
by making yourself tired or diverted. If you can't get rid of
that rage, just clench your teeth and smile. People will soon
get the picture and keep out of your way.

Your Ex Took All of Your Stuff
Don't worry, you've still got your health!

You can say, "I lost everything." You can say, "I have nothing." Many have said these words after a separation where their partner took all of their material goods and left them with virtually nothing. It's a difficult thing to face and when someone has left us, we say those words with anguish, and there's nothing worse than anguish. Just poverty. Or despondency. Or being very very cold.

Legal Thievery
Grease up and take advantage of your friend

The Tale of Charles

How would you describe heaven? Imagine a beautiful big white mansion in the Nevada desert with an incredible outdoor recreation area. Beautifully landscaped rock pools on five different levels produce mini waterfalls that cascade elegantly from one pool to the next, like a champagne glass fountain at a royal wedding. Palm trees form natural sun umbrellas with shady leaves and are surrounded by pink California honeysuckle and tiny white and yellow European roses. Imported glossy blue and white tiles form a moat where multicolored fish swim inside, as mini watchmen of the property. Even bees with uncharacteristic melodic buzzing are brought in from a distant rainforest and introduced into the garden. They are so well-mannered that they never sting anyone without asking first.

Elizabeth and Charles had such a house and indulgent oasis. Their place was so big and lovely that they wanted to show it off and share it with other people. After all, why have such a great place and keep it to yourself? So they had parties on the weekends and lots of beautiful impressionable young people came, and they were impressed. The young women bathed and drank and danced outside under the hot sun in thong bikinis and young men swam and flirted and were covered in oil. And everyone glowed because it was everyone's piece of heaven while they were allowed to be there.

Elizabeth and Charles were always over-achievers. They each ran their own businesses and were incredibly successful. But the more you have the more you want, and the more you get, the more someone wants a piece of that, too. Or even all of it, because that's what some people are like: greedy.

How would you describe hell? Not having everything you want? Wrong. The devil plays his own game. You have everything you want and life is perfect. Then one day it is all taken away from you. And that's hell. Well it certainly was for Charles. While he was away on one of his frequent business trips, Elizabeth found herself falling for an oily young man who had given her some attention at one of their parties, along with his greasy, oil-covered phone number. They were two of a kind, a conniving kind, and between them they formed one gigantic scheming criminal mind and were able to take Charles for everything he had. Now bereft of his belongings, Charles was then officially poor and had lost everything he cared about, including his marriage.

Illegal Thievery
Equestrian breakage is a bitter pill to swallow

The Tale of Raymond

Raymond and Becky rented a small house on Hickory Street, in a suburban area of Florence, Kentucky. They were happy together for several years, living a simple life and making an honest living. They each looked forward to their weekends, spending Saturdays at the racetrack together and Sundays with Becky's family. Sadly, they grew apart and for a reason no one will ever know, they lost interest in being together. This avoidance was never mentioned; they just started spending their free time without each other. Ray went to the track alone and Becky would visit her parents.

Becky was a controlling lady, round-faced and red-cheeked but her kindly look was the reverse of her character. She decided that because Ray no longer served a useful purpose in her life she would put him to work. She signed him up for a landscaping job with a neighbor's business so that he could bring home more money to spend on her. She had already put a new faux fur winter coat on layaway for both herself and a matching one for Tammi, her little pooch, and she needed Ray to pay for them both.

Ray had to work weekdays on his first job and weekends on his second job, so his free time was as hard to find as a margarita stand at an AA meeting. Mostly he missed watching the horses race, but instead he listened to the races on a headset while he cut grass in the summer. The first snow-shoveling Christmas that Ray had to work, Becky thoughtfully gave him a ceramic racehorse and he decided to start a collection. With the little money he had left over from his job after the dog and wife had taken their cut (or coat), he began buying replicas of famous racehorses. Even though it didn't compare to watching the real thing, after a while he had built up his racehorse collection to over 45 ceramic, pottery, bronze and plastic racehorses. His favorite was a large plastic replica of Gimme More, a tan thoroughbred who had won a million dollar purse at the Kentucky Downs in 1996.

It was only a matter of time until Becky found another man to bully. It was Ralph, from Ralph's Supershop and Dry Goods ("The Best in Town, Guaranteed!"). Ralph was a sly businessman and within a few months he had moved Becky out of her small marital house and into his Supershop-sized house. Between them, they took everything from Ray and Becky's old house, and because Ray couldn't pay the rent by himself, he had to move out.

The day Becky left with Ralph, Ray came home from work and found the locks were changed. The new tenants had already bagged up Ray's racehorse collection that Becky had left behind in a plastic baggie, that was ironically from Ralph's Supershop and Dry Goods ("The Best in Town, Guaranteed!") and left it on top of the garbage cans for Saturday's pick up. It was a shame. Many of the horses were broken because fragile animals such as racehorses shaken together inside a plastic bag do not get along with each other. The horse wars that ensued had left many casualties, not to mention many pieces. Ray rode away on his bicycle in the pouring rain, the horses clattering together in the baggie balanced on his handlebars, almost making the sound of a gallop, but in fact, making more pieces of each other. Ray wondered how it had ever come to this. He was then officially poor and had lost everything he cared about, including his marriage.

Comment

After a relationship breaks up, material possessions are divided between the parties, sometimes fairly, sometimes not. Some may lose things they worked hard to acquire or that they cared about. It may be a mansion or a ceramic racehorse collection, but we consider it to be our "stuff" and we don't want to give it up. It's another notch of loss on the whittled stick of breakup and companions the bitter taste of abandonment. Why should the one who did no wrong be punished again after their partner leaves them for a conniving, oily-torsoed Adonis or a businessman with the dull glint of deception in his eye? Whether you lost millions of dollars or dozens, you could each end up with the loser's prize in the reality game show of *Loser Loses All*.

So then comes the time after you have licked the salty wounds of defeat, that you start thinking about building it all back up again. Some want more because it's human nature to want more and they are driven by determination and anger to become financially successful. Others are tired of building, and find solace in the little that remains. Peace and acceptance are now in their lives and they are content living with only a few material goods. Their living rooms may be sparsely furnished with a folding chair and a sturdy plastic crate for a table or a shelf, but that's what's good about life in the civilized part of the world. You can work hard to buy more, or you can stay with the basic things in life, if that's what makes you happy.

But also, the man with little can change his mind and make his first million, inspired by a badly glued ceramic racehorse collection and a large plastic indestructible Gimme More. The striving businessman may turn to a frugal life and discover that the folding chair can be quite comfortable and they come in a range of creative colors. The plastic crates are fairly easy to come by and you can stack them as high as you like! You see, there's always something to learn, even for the most educated of people, and it's never too late to turn your life around.

Why Does My Ex Hate Me?
Is that our *f r i e n d s h i p* flying out the window?

Your breakup was amicable, but then out of the blue your ex starts treating you like gum under a shoe; a chewed-out irritation that's lost its flavor. They seem to hate you and stop returning your calls, or maybe they do something hurtful. What's that all about? Weren't you recently in bed together, whispering, "I love you, baby," all over the place?

The Tale of Zoe

Women can feel inadequate about their looks after a breakup and they may be misled into thinking a new look will entice their loved ones back to them. More often than not it's an unreasonable thought, because the breakup was probably due to them not getting along, and not about their looks. But some women wouldn't agree.

Zoe was optimistic that she and her husband, Liam, would reunite. All it would take would be for him to see her new look and he would fall in love with her all over again. Her plan was to buy new clothes and shoes, and to try some creative makeup to entice him. She had her hair cut to perfection and every day she was dressed kill in case she ran into him. She had even practiced her walk, which had become a cross between a flounce and a wiggle. It was perfect.

On a non-descript Thursday in October she received a joint credit card bill in the mail, which was strange, because she thought she and Liam had canceled all of the credit cards they had together. This must be one they had missed. It showed only one charge, which was to a jewelry store for a large amount of money plus a late fee. That's odd, she thought, but then it occurred to her that Liam must be going to surprise her and ask her to come back to him. Not only that, but he had bought her an expensive piece of jewelry to show how sorry he was for breaking up with her! Excited by the thought of a reunion with bling, she stopped at the jewelry store to discover what he had picked out for her.

The manager remembered the sale well, and when he told her it was for a diamond engagement ring, it was indeed a surprise. Zoe was puzzled. Liam had already bought her an engagement ring before they were married. Why would he buy her another one? The manager listened to her logic, and afterward, very diplomatically, told her that the bride-to-be had stopped by only yesterday with her fiancé Mr. Liam, to pick up the ring. The wedding was to be in the summer of the following year.

Zoe felt faint and everything went out of focus. The manager had to ask the watch battery replacement girl, Katy, to fetch a chair for her. He then had to ask Katy to fetch a glass of water for her. Then there was a line of people needing watch batteries, so the manager had to bring her an aspirin himself. Zoe felt small and deflated. Not only would there be no flouncing up to her ex-husband in her cherry-red stilettos, but there would be no admiration of how great she looked in her new outfit. The most salt was rubbed into the engagement ring wound—she couldn't believe he was getting engaged, and his new girlfriend would make out like the bandit that she was. Another wife! He was getting married again and they weren't even divorced yet. It was heartbreaking.

Once she arrived home she called the credit card company to remove her name from the charge, but they told her that they were unable to do so. They said the charge card was in both of their names and she or Liam would be responsible to pay the bill as the goods had been collected. "Well," she retorted, furiously, "I'll make sure that he pays the whole bill."

"That might be a good idea, Ma'am," responded the credit card company representative, "because if he won't pay, you are liable for the whole amount."

Zoe was appalled. It was inconceivable that she would have to pay for Liam's fiancée's engagement ring! She didn't even know that he had a girlfriend, and besides, her own engagement ring had only cost half as much! She immediately called Liam, but he wouldn't pick up the phone or return her calls. After feeling sick to her stomach, she felt horrified, betrayed and hurt. Then she felt enraged, murderous and revengeful. Then she sat down and poured herself a stiff drink and fell asleep in the big armchair.

It's a wild story that has a compelling soap-opera ending. The very next day Zoe's wish to accidentally bump into Liam came true at the car wash. Her beautiful new clothes were left at home and were impressing all of her old clothes in the closet, along with the cherry-red patent leather shoes. The flounce was forgotten and her walk was more gorilla than girl. There was murder lurking in her eyes and the new makeup was also noticeably absent. Liam took a step back when he saw her. The lack of make-up on her face and scant two hours of sleep enhanced the dark circles under her eyes, and they reminded Liam of the eye black that football players wear to intimidate the opposing team. The clothes she wore were gang-bang baggy sweats, making her look twice her normal size and inmate-like menacing. She had planned for weeks to look her best for him, but now she looked more like a bouncer than a flouncer. Liam shook in his shoes at this vision of dreadfulness as she clomped towards him, waving a chamois carwash cloth that splashed dirty water onto his suit. Afraid for his life, he stepped backward over a bucket of grimy water and slipped into a pile of dirty wet rags that were stacked for the laundry. Once upon a time there was a fairy tale romance, but where was the prince now? Lying on his back in a pile of wet and dirty rags at the Monroe Street Car Wash!

Comment

Why does our ex turn against us for seemingly no reason? Is it because they hate us? Not always, but it's the first rationale in our minds. Maybe we should shift the blame to that heartless, self-centered partner-stealer, who said to our ex, "Lookie here Dale, I don't want you seeing that good-fer-nuthin' ex of yours again." *That's* the perfect person to blame, but that might not be what happened.

After a breakup, people behave in different ways toward each other because many emotions are involved. It is difficult to psychoanalyze your ex's behavior. The Yin is fighting with the Yang and just when you think you know which end is up, you discover that it's the wrong end. It's mystifying when your ex starts ignoring you out of the blue or does something hurtful for no reason. You can over-analyze all of the reasons why, but ultimately, the solution may only be found in a pack of Tarot cards or a crystal ball. Their behavior defies all rational logic. We are all familiar with the phrase, "They broke up with me, but now they won't even return my phone calls. What did I do wrong?" Probably nothing, apart from existing and unknowingly making them feel guilty because they broke up with you. They may still care about you and feel responsible about hurting you, even though they are happily jumping into bed with Ruby, or Theo the landscaper.

Your only recourse is to test the waters. When your ex is being hostile or vindictive, first look behind you, to make sure they are not standing there with a sharpened butcher's knife, and if it's safe, take a step backward to give them some space. If possible, leave them alone for a while, and let them make the first move in contacting you.

If they are ignoring you, maybe they just have other things on their mind or they need some time away from you to let everyone's feelings settle like dust in the guestroom. They may have decided to cut all ties with you. Now that it's over, you may be the street that they have turned the corner on. It's not always easy to know what they are thinking, even after all of the history you had together. Also, it goes without saying, if children or debts are involved, you will have a real problem on your hands and legal help is your best remedy.

Still, none of this helps your hurt feelings at the moment. Again the anger-guilt-anger theory rears its ugly head and becomes a vicious cycle that's best ridden away on. Unfortunately, you, the hurt party, is hurt again when your ex turns his or her back on you, or harms you. And a hurt party ain't much of a party at all. In fact, partying might be just the way for you to go in order to forget about your ex, who is still running like a mad bull through all of your thoughts.

As for Liam, he might not have been thinking ahead when he bought the ring, not realizing his action could implicate Zoe. Or maybe he had no money, but wanted to keep or impress his new girl. He may just have been stupid. Or really really smart, and we could guess all day long why he did it; and if it's a rainy day with a chill wind blowing and there are a few caramels left in the birthday box, it might be a good way to pass the time.

Coping and Adjusting

It's a bright, sunny day and you are walking by the river when suddenly you hear someone calling out. You peer into the distance and see someone waving to you from the water with both arms up in the air. They disappear under the water for a moment, then reappear and start waving frantically again and they are calling out to you. It sounds like they are calling out "Bill," or "Nell," or "help," or something like that. To be polite, you wave back, even though your name isn't Bill or Nell. You put the incident out of your mind and when you arrive home, it suddenly hits you! Oh my God, that person could be you after your breakup, struggling in your newly-single life! It's just like the floundering right before you learn to swim. You get a little water in your ears, your hair drips, and you have moments when you think you are drowning, but you dog-paddle along in your new home.

Men and women have different roles in life, even though everyone tries to deny it. Women are burdened with cooking and cleaning, and they suffer the agony of giving birth; men are burdened with car repair and heavy lifting, and suffer the agony of deciding which game to watch on television tonight. When you split from your partner, you have to take over the opposite sex role, as well as continuing to do those things you have always done. It can be tricky; it can be intimidating; and it can be pretty damn tiring.

Coping for Women
Misleading Predators 101

Women have different obstacles to overcome than men when they are newly alone. Initially, it can be a time of fear because the security and strength of a man is gone. For example, if you hear a prowler in the middle of night, there's no one to nudge with your icy foot and say "Hey! Hector! Wake up. There's someone in the kitchen! Here's a nail file to use as a weapon. Go down there and toss him out!" Even if you are a powerful, strong woman, you are most likely not as strong as a man, and security fears can come in various forms.

The Tale of Nancy

Nancy was a 5 foot 8 inches tall broad-shouldered tough woman who most men wouldn't want to mess with, but she was cautious because she had been raised street-wise and knew how dangerous people can be (even the short, skinny ones). After Harrison moved out of their apartment, she felt vulnerable and was prone to panic attacks. One evening she heard noises in her home that sounded like zombies in the next room, mumbling something about "brains," but when she mentioned it to her neighbor, she laughed at her and said it must have been the sound of her hairdryer, right before it went on the fritz. A week later she was awakened from a deep sleep when someone knocked loudly on her front door at 3 a.m., calling out in a drunken drawl, "Adele! Adele! Wake up, honey, I'm home!" and she said to herself "enough is enough."

The very next morning she went out and bought the biggest pair of men's work boots that she could find. She took some mud from the yard and spread it on them, making them look used and tough, and she put them outside her apartment door. Now the prowlers and zombies would think that a man with big feet and matching muscles lived there, and wouldn't come knocking on her door in the early hours of the morning, calling her Adele.

She was mistrustful of her mechanic when she brought her car in. She thought he might convince her to have some unnecessary work done on her vehicle, so she bought a gold-colored cheapo wedding ring that looked like the real thing and wore it on her wedding finger when she brought her car in to be fixed. That way the mechanic would think she had a big, hairy, tough husband at home who would lean on him if he tried to sell her something that her car didn't need. Or even a little husband with a hairless body and anger issues. You can never tell with husbands until you get to really know them.

The message on her answering machine was in the plural "we can't come to the phone right now…" so that callers wouldn't know that she lived alone. When she went hiking in the woods she wore a large shapeless jacket and held her keys in her hand as a chunky weapon, ready to wave threateningly at potential rapists, because everyone knows that rapists live and breed in the woods. (She was lucky that she never met a rapist, because he may have thought the waving of the keys was an offer to take him home.) As a safety precaution, a friend suggested she put an inflatable man doll in her car or her living room window, to make it look like she had a boyfriend, but she decided that was going too far, and anyway, those men were ugly and they probably smelled of plastic.

Comment

Life can be difficult for a woman living alone, especially after she has been used to the company and protection of a man. Women have historically been labeled many things in the past—the weaker sex, the fairer sex, and so on. Although these phrases are now moot due to evolution and women's rights, men may still think women too weak to open a door for themselves as they enter a room, especially if they are balancing a small child on each hip and carrying a frozen thanksgiving turkey in a backpack.

But you can't argue with the fact that although women may be tough, often their size and physical strength is less than that of a man. A female alone can be prey to a man looking for easy money or easy sex, and if any women out there are saying, "Oh, that just sounds like a typical man," you may be harboring just a little too much resentment. Maybe now's the time for you to give up the real thing and go for the blow-up type.

Coping for Men
Slaying the Household Monsters

*M*en typically, but not always, have to adjust to taking care of their home after a breakup. They may have found in the past that their significant other took care of this issue, but now it's up to them to add another job to the nine to five, with virtually no training.

The Tale of Phil

Phil had been raised by a mother who catered to his every whim. He was the little prince of the family and between his three sisters and his mother, neither he nor his father ever had to lift a finger to prepare a meal, grocery shop or clean the house. Their "job" was to drink beer at night in front of the TV and fix the car if it broke down.

So when Phil and Tina moved in together, Phil always counted on Tina, his long-time girlfriend to take care of all issues related to the apartment, while he concentrated on work and maintaining the car. He never helped with the housework or the laundry, and he had never ever grocery shopped. Phil had lived in the same place with Tina for three years, and now that she had moved out, the home was a stranger to him. He knew there was a room off the dining room where Tina used to spend a lot of time. It was from this room that she would emerge with sumptuous meals for them: roast turkeys, pies, stir fries—all manner of foods. But it had been at least a year since he stepped into The Kitchen.

Tina had left him four months ago and since then, he had eaten every meal out or had take-out brought in. But late one Sunday night, with the hail and wind whipping around the windows, he decided to venture into The Kitchen. Standing alone in that unfamiliar room he felt like he was in someone else's home. There was a door leading off from The Kitchen. How was it that he had never seen that door before? It was like one of those movies where the inquisitive teenager finds a room in the house that leads to a crazy relative who has been living in there for 25 years without anyone else knowing. He tried the door, it wasn't locked, but it creaked eerily when he opened it. It was pitch black inside and he hurriedly flicked on the light.

Despite his height and weight, he took a step back, his heart pounding. There were two huge machines in there, both glaringly white and shiny. They looked familiar, but for a second he couldn't place them in his mind. Then it came to him as an epiphany—a washer and a dryer! It was amazing what undiscovered marvels could be found in strange rooms in your own apartment. That meant he could do laundry without leaving his home! How great was that? He closed the door, turned off the light and suddenly noticed a really bad smell in the air. Where was it coming from? It seemed to be emanating from a bulky, dark green container of some sort, standing tall from floor almost to ceiling. Well, even Phil knew that it was a refrigerator, because that's where the beer was kept. But why was there a bad smell coming from it? And what was that green slime that seemed to be dripping from the door? There must be food in it (good guess, Phil). Maybe it was over four months old…

So that Sunday night, Phil undertook a non-denominational domestic cleansing. He rolled up his sleeves, took out a heavy duty garbage bag, reached for the bleach and cleaned not only the fridge, but also the entire kitchen. In a matter of days he was cooking, cleaning, and even ironing after he did the laundry. The fridge had never been so spotless and was filled with fresh food every other month (let's not get too crazy here)!

Comment

We become complacent in our relationships and after a while our roles are determined and habits are set. Someone pays the bills while the other person cooks or grocery shops. When you find yourself alone, all of the household jobs will fall upon your shoulders. That's a heavy burden to carry, so if you find your shoulders are not strong enough, you have to start weight training. This can be done by shopping and using both hands to carry the groceries, scrubbing the paintwork until it shines, vacuuming the staircase and painting the ceiling. That's one of the perks about living alone; you get a two for one. Not only will your home be sparkling clean, you'll be fit and healthy. Not to mention all the money you'll save on a gym membership.

It's Holiday Time
Let's all be miserable!

veryone loves a parade, or so the old song goes. It's a bit of myth, really, like Santa Claus and being told that vegetables are good for you. Holidays, when you are newly single, are nothing but a trap, even though many of them feature parades. You are expecting a holiday to be fun, because after all, it's time off from work or at least it's a time for celebration. Besides the parades, there are family parties, gatherings with friends and loved ones and even some romantic moments. Like many other events when you are single, you will have to rethink holidays. Being alone can be full of dangerous things lurking around the corner that are not always identified by a ski mask and a weapon sticking out of a back pocket. But these dangerous things can also throw you into the depths of despair. One of them is country and western music and the other is holidays. Christmas, Memorial Day, Thanksgiving and New Year are all dangerous holidays, but the baddest daddy of them all is Valentine's Day.

The Tale of Lucy

Lucy had loved Valentine's Day since kindergarten, when the kids cut out red hearts and glued them onto cards for their moms. At that tender age you are already becoming a victim of greeting cards' holidays and are being indoctrinated into the belief that if you don't participate, you are not loved. As she grew older, Lucy believed Valentine's Day was a necessary romantic fantasy, second only to the ultimate fantasy, The Wedding Day. But this year, Valentine's Day was to be a non-event for poor Lucy. She was alone this year and was loveless, lonely and lost. Since Sean had found love somewhere else, she was counting with dread the days that led up to February 14th.

She wandered into the drugstore right after New Year's Day to buy a birthday card. She had forgotten it was the time when the Valentine's Day goods climbed onto the shelves, rubbing the New Year's hangover from their eyes. There it all was, the musical cards with their falsetto voices; the heart-shaped boxes of chocolates; the stuffed toys with their oversized eyes and lips; and the most taunting item of all, the hollow chocolate, extra large, red foil-wrapped heart. An innocent visit to buy a card resulted in her coming home with her eyes bloodshot and itchy from seeing all of that scarlet merchandise, forcing her to use eye drops to take out the red.

Two weeks later, the Valentine's Day made-for-TV movies had begun and romance was excreted from every television channel with promises of new love, happiness and laughter. Interspersed between the movies were the jewelry commercials, sparkles of gold and gems encouraging even the most masculine women to dress up like girlie-girls and persuading them to discard the leather and studs for a day. While the diamonds sparkled under their special lights, they promised love everlasting, the bigger the stone the better the love, and every girl knew that to be true.

Television became too depressing for Lucy, so one evening after work she went to the mall for some retail calming of the soul. It turned out to be a bad idea, as the storefronts were all dressed up for their big Valentine's Day promotions. At the lingerie store, the mannequins were already dressed up in their sexiest outfits, unwittingly enticing the male mannequins from the Big and Tall store across the way, who leered at them with unblinking eyes. Once in the store, the salesgirls descended on her like flies to a whipped cream bikini, and she fought them off with glares and elbows. They questioned her about her boyfriend, and when she admitted to having lost one, they bullied her into thinking that because she was so careless, she didn't deserve to be sexy, and then they banished her to the back of the store. Those carefree witches all had boyfriends!

There she found a world she never knew existed. It was the place where women of every shape and size, over a size 4, bought their undergarments, hidden from the critical view of the young, sexy and in love. Women of all ages without boyfriends or husbands formed a sisterhood of normal shapes, the way God had made them. Elderly ladies were also gathered back there, buying grandmamma underwear with thick, yellowing waistbands, their chatter whispering all around her like a moth inside her ear. As Lucy picked out a below-the-knee slip, she asked a friendly shopper who was standing nearby, "Do you always hide in the back when you buy underwear from here?" The lady smiled and shook her head.

"No. Only in the month of February," she sighed. It was almost as secretive as a drug deal, Lucy thought to herself as she paid, looking over her shoulder to make sure no one she knew came into the store. Is this what it's like to be single on Valentine's Day?

At the beginning of February, she bumped into her neighbor, Arnold, and they began chatting and laughing about her pre-Valentine's day experiences. He agreed that the Valentine's Day world was indeed difficult and depressing, and he was more than understanding. He, too, had broken up with his love, Sandy, and for five years had successfully avoided Valentine's Day. They decided to join forces and together they planned their escape from February 14th. As an army of two they stormed the drug stores and fought the evil red confection together, buying only candy and chocolate in its original street-clothes wrappers. They purchased DVDs online that were dramas and action movies, ignoring the romances and the comedies where love stories ran rampant through them like seed through a lovebird, and they stockpiled them. Grocery shopping was done together in bulk, wine and food was brought into their homes and the radio was boxed up and stored in the closet.

While Valentine's Day was swinging its magnet of merchandising around, Lucy and Arnold were protected from chocolate boxes with hearts and cherubs; from romantic movies on television, and commercials for the terminally in-love. Arnold had helped Lucy avoid the mall with its lingerie-baited storefronts and that vicious beast, the card shop was now curbed. They had wine to drown their sorrows, food to divert the soul, movies to distract them and that other dangerous beast, the radio, with its love songs, dedications and country music was out of sight and out of mind. And so they were saved for another year.

Comment

It is not necessary to have a Valentine's Day buddy for that day. Being alone is fine if you follow Arnold's advice. This advice can be used for any holiday and when the day comes, you are protected inside your own home. You don't even need to lock the door. The day after Valentine's Day when you venture confidently out, you will see that people who expected gifts, flowers or fancy dinners, will have lost that 14th glow. Most will have a curse: a hangover, food poisoning, an unwanted pregnancy or a falling out with their partner because they were disappointed that their diamonds turned out to be cubic zirconia. February 15th is a great day for single people to gloat, plus you can pick up all kinds of good quality candy for half price, and enjoy smashing up that hollow chocolate, extra large, red foil-wrapped heart with your fist and then stuffing the chocolate into your mouth, without having to share it with anyone. Abstaining from other holidays also have their benefits: no sunstroke in the summer on Memorial Day; no egg allergies at Easter; no pie baking stress for Thanksgiving and think of all of the money you can save on holiday gift buying if you hang out by yourself at Christmas or Hanukkah. And New Year's Eve? ALWAYS an anticlimax.

Bewildered

Dating in an unfamiliar wonderland

o you remember when you were young and you rode the merry-go-round? Some children loved it, others became dizzy and either fell off or threw up. Whichever child you were, that's not relevant here. What *is* relevant is the memory of it. When the carousel first began moving slowly around, right before you waved to your dad, you felt a little disoriented. You and your horse, Ned, moved at a slow speed, while the real world continued around you at a normal pace. It can feel a little like that when you are suddenly single. You may be functioning at 65% of your usual capacity, stumbling along in circles and trying to remember all the fresh things life now consists of. Because the old habits have been castrated, familiar things are either hard to find or gone. Besides paying your own bills, fixing your own meals and changing the filter on the air conditioning unit, you are meeting new people. You may have a new girlfriend or boyfriend.

The Tale of Andy

Andy found his routine severely disrupted when his marriage of 35 years broke up, because life with Sadie had moved along smoothly while they were still together, and it was a life of peace and predictability. But when Sadie left him, he was thrown into a confusion that made him feel like a monkey at the zoo, with people pointing at him and saying things he couldn't understand. His memory was not what it used to be and his housekeeping skills were zero. He found it hard to eat anything because he was accustomed to the meals that Sadie cooked and nothing else appealed to him. People confused him, and when he met someone new he would forget their face by the next time he met them. His life was in turmoil and adding dating to that equation was just inviting more problems that would involve new information to process and retain. But, being a normal man, his libido sent him out searching for a replacement mate and it told him not to come back until he found one.

His first new girlfriend after his wife left was Mimi, and she became the guinea pig in Andy's experiment of "Less Bewildering Dating." Much to Mimi's annoyance, he kept calling her by the name of his ex-wife, Sadie. This was becoming a problem because Mimi was also getting confused. So Andy decided to call her just Baby, which sounded somewhat like "Mimi," especially if you were a little deaf in the left ear, as Mimi was. Once the relationship with Mimi ended, other girlfriends followed and the generic Honey or Darling were added to Andy's repertoire of endearing names. That was one more thing he didn't need to think about and as a first step, it was helpful.

As girlfriends came and went, his dating experiment progressed, as did his prowess in all things girlfriend generic. He went shopping and bought two dozen of last season's red berets, which he kept hidden in his closet. As each new female came into his life, he would gift each one a brand new red beret and tell them how good they looked in it. This thrilled them, because it made him look thoughtful and generous, and it was helpful to him if he couldn't find anything else that was complimentary to say about them. But Andy had an ulterior motive—if they were out together at the movies, the mall or the grocery store and she wandered off, he didn't need to stop and think, "Who am I with at the moment?" He just needed to look for the red beret. It made shopping and dating much easier for him and he never tried to take the wrong woman home again. (That *was* an embarrassing evening.)

Once organized, Andy went to the next step, which was date teaching. He would lend each new girlfriend Sadie's old recipe book, where all of his favorite recipes were highlighted. He encouraged his girlfriends to cook Sadie's meals and miraculously his appetite returned, and his interest in food was back to where it was during his marriage. He even became a little overweight! He then taught each girlfriend his original sex moves that he and his ex-wife used, and sex once again became the routine, predictable activity it had been with Sadie. Abracadabra! His life was almost back to the way it was when he was married, so he hardly had to think ahead at all.

Comment

As we age, it becomes more difficult to give up the routine we had with our partners. Our brains are so full of the past, that it's hard to cram new things in without something that's important slipping out. So now it's all about making things easy for ourselves. Make lists. Use calendars you can write on. Try to keep things in the same routine as much as possible, which puts less stress on your life. It's not easy, but it's also no picnic for someone young, either.

But be a friend to yourself and be tolerant of your brain; it also needs some kindness as it struggles with its heavy load of information, wit and experiences. This is how nature put us together and very little can help our memory improve, except for a large glass of water from the fountain of youth, and if you know where that is, don't forget to share the knowledge. It's really not so bad because everyone is in it together, and your new date should be sympathetic of that fact, unless they are more than a decade younger than you are, and if that's the case, you are already lucky—so don't push it!

So who said divorce and adjusting to another mate is difficult? Be like Andy and just don't tell them your little secret. Keep watching the same shows on television that you used to watch during your marriage, go to the same restaurants, name all of your dogs the same and before you know it, you'll be back where you started. See how easy your life can be? It's hardly changing at all.

Hating Your Ex

The metamorphosis from hate to abate

You have been dumped and you are angry. Changes are going on inside you, and you can feel yourself metamorphosing into something unknown because hate starts to eat you up from inside. It grows big and fat, like a caterpillar at the larva stage eating its way through stacks of leaves. But be careful, instead of following an instinct to destruction like the caterpillar, use the six rules of hate control below as a guide on how to keep yourself out of trouble.

Keeping Yourself in Check When You Want to Harm Your Ex: The Six Rules of Conduct

RULE ONE: No person shall destroy material possessions of another that may cause interference with that person's enjoyment of life.

Just because you know your ex really well and you know where to hit for maximum impact, doesn't mean you can destroy or steal their stuff. This includes pulling out wires to electronics and hiding their chargers. So make a list of all of the revengeful things you could do, fold the list six times and stuff it into a pillow. It may sound like voodoo to you, but without the chicken feathers and virgin's blood it isn't; but it will make you feel a whole lot better without leaving a trail of destruction behind you.

RULE TWO: The incitement of a riot is forbidden. To that end, if more than five persons gather outside of a residence, they will be construed as an angry mob and be removed.

Rule Two disallows the rounding up of your friends in order to bad-talk your ex. This kind of meeting can incite anger and before you know it, you and your friends have hopped into your car and driven to your ex's home at 2 a.m. You have congregated outside their front door like a posse of gunslingers, whistling and jeering and calling out to them "come out of the house you yellow-bellied snake." Not a good thing for anyone to wake up to. It may also affect the value of their real estate.

RULE THREE: Cyber revenge will not be tolerated, nor will the posting of indecent materials on the Internet.

Online revenge may not seem as bad to you as inflicting physical revenge or harm, but mental anguish is right up there with a black eye. Cyber payback is a no-no and blogging, tweeting, chatting and posting offensive remarks about your breakup online is something you may soon regret. Posting hideous pictures of your ex online also is forbidden under Rule Three, because a photograph is just a silent word. This also goes for posting pics of you with your new love dancing naked in the rain. Not cool.

RULE FOUR: No person shall be allowed to incite anger to another, when it may initiate a destructive chain of causation.

Number Four warns you about hanging out with bad friends. These people will rile you up and make you angry and your hate will rise up like over-yeasted bread. Then where will *they* be when you are out trying to buy a gun on the bad side of town? Fast asleep in their beds, that's where. So be watchful when you are with your friends, because you may not notice right away that what they say to you can make you become angry with your ex. Does Nate incite hate? Does Jack provoke payback? Mary make you wary? Angie make you angry? Unfortunately, people's names are not usually an indication of their behavior, but if you become angrier when you are with them, just tell Guy, "bye-bye."

RULE FIVE: It is against the rules to make libelous remarks, besmirch another person's good character, or to slander the good reputation or integrity of another individual.

When women talk, it's gossip, when men talk, it's conversation, but whatever you call it, watch what you say. Talking bad about your ex to your friends makes you look like the bad one, and your friends may not like this once-hidden, vindictive side of you. After all, they may think if you say insulting things about your ex, what are you saying about them behind their backs? Words are like e-mails or pinless grenades, you can't take them back.

RULE SIX: The infliction of actual bodily harm or killing of ex-partners will not be tolerated under any circumstances.

Hate is a slow-release emotion and the only way to rid yourself of it quickly is to eliminate the source. Murder is illegal in most countries of the world, so if you don't murder your ex, their new partner, their parents or their best friends Alvin and Lilly, congratulations! You have just passed number six and completed the test!

Comment

The chain of hate runs: anger, hate, revenge, violence, anger. It's a circle like the one in the action dramas where the hero stands in the middle and takes on the bad guys one at a time. It's dangerous in that circle and you should avoid it at all costs. You don't know how your ex is feeling or what kind of retaliation they may consider if you "do them wrong," so don't do it. Your hate will slowly drain out in time and you will be your kindly self again. But meanwhile, grit your teeth and have your neighbor take care of your kitchen knives until you calm down. It's hate in the red corner and restraint and a guiltless night's sleep in the blue. So pick a corner and hunker down.

Regular Sex
What time does the sex mobile come by?
I need to get me some

You were accustomed to regular sex if you were in a normal relationship. This could be something you will miss once you are single. You are no longer getting it on tap like draft beer and if you want it, you will have to look for it. Sometimes it comes to you like a gift without a ribbon and sometimes it's impossible to find, like cheap flowers on Valentine's Day. People get comfortable in their sexual relationships and it's difficult to start over with a newcomer (no pun intended).

The lists below show that:

One: People eventually adapt to losing the benefit of regular sex;

Two: They compare new sex to the old sex;

Three: They find out if their routines and quirks were affected;

Four: They discover things about their urges;

Five: Their stress levels are affected; and so on.

The two lists below indicate how some newly-single people cope with the loss of regular sex in a relationship.

They are categorized into female (She) and male (He) stereotypes. Feel free to interchange them:

SHE:

> was happy to end her marital obligations.
>
> now had more time for the ironing in her busy schedule.
>
> enjoyed it more with someone else.
>
> missed the foreplay and the afterglow the most.
>
> discovered that every man has a different technique.
>
> stopped shaving her legs and underarms.
>
> realized the only time she used to listen to music was during sex.
>
> felt that abstinence created a heat she didn't know she had.
>
> found out she preferred women.
>
> believed that if she wasn't picky, she could always get lucky.
>
> discovered online "friends."
>
> started going out alone at night to bars.
>
> didn't have to worry anymore about getting pregnant.
>
> missed the smell of a man.
>
> bought a bag of toys.
>
> began to lose her temper more quickly.
>
> wondered why her friends didn't sympathize.
>
> paid less on her lingerie bills.
>
> took to wearing sweat suits.
>
> became moody and irritable.
>
> was afraid she may never have sex again.

HE:

> realized that casual sex was hard to come by.
>
> cancelled one of his more expensive prescriptions.
>
> bought a slew of girlie movies and magazines.

was more stressed.

couldn't live a day without it.

believed it was the same wherever he got it.

was lonely without someone lying next to him.

discovered female telephone "friends."

missed the creative acts of his kinky and perverse ex-partner.

discovered that bodies all felt different.

was told that his blood pressure was up.

was used to the old routine of Tuesday, Friday and Sunday.

found out his life was never inspired again.

did not need to shower as often.

felt sex with anyone besides his ex-partner was just "going through the motions."

was worried that a hiatus would render him impotent.

missed the softness of a woman.

knew his friends really sympathized.

stopped wearing his black underwear.

found himself strangely aroused by certain television commercials.

was afraid he may never have sex again.

Comment

Some people miss sex and some are glad it's over. There's a proverb that says, "A change is as good as a rest," so if there's suddenly no sex, it's a change, and that can be good for some people. For others, it's like what they say about Chinese food, "No sooner are you satisfied by it, then you are ready for more," and that's why committed relationships can be a good thing. So apply one of those sayings to yourself, or make up your own. After all, if you're not having sex anymore, think of all the free time you'll have.

Don't Talk to Me
How to kill the kindness of others

There's nothing worse than someone trying to be helpful when you are upset or in a bad mood. The most annoying people will generally be older than you and have an infuriating knowing look in their eyes. They will nod like a bobblehead Elvis and say to you, "I've been there, you know." Well, much as you'd like to tell them to go back there, you will have to listen to them say their piece, and they pretty much all say the same things.

"Don't worry, you'll get over it."

Not helpful at this stage. It's the kind of thing you can only understand by biding your time, healing and then actually getting over them, but do you believe it now? Will you believe it next week? Unlikely. It's like saying do you want $50 now or $5,000 in twenty years? When you are feeling wretched, you want instant gratification, not a promise of something that might be a mile or two down the road. So don't let them tell you that you will feel better sometime in the future, unless they are clairvoyant and can tell you the exact day it will happen. The best advice is to lay low until you feel strong enough to emerge.

"Stop feeling sorry for yourself."

Self pity is an underrated emotion, and because it's an emotion, it should be accepted. Don't let people tell you to stop feeling sorry for yourself. If God didn't want us to feel sorry for ourselves, he wouldn't have put the feeling sorry area in our brain, right between the frontal lobe and the hippocampus. Look it up on a brain map—it's there right next to the overeating and hypochondria areas. And it's yours to use whenever you want it. After all, it's your brain.

"Don't worry about your break up—there are plenty more fish in the sea."

It's a known fact that there are many different kinds of fish in the sea and most of them don't get along with each other. I bet it takes a fish a long time to meet another fish it actually likes but doesn't want to devour. Anyway, most fish don't have relationships. They don't even mate. The female lays the eggs and the males drop their bits on them and then they swim away. So you just tell those people the truth about the fish and ask them, "What do you think of your fish in the sea now? Not looking so romantic anymore are they?"

"I told you so."

Who feels better when this is said? Your enemy of the moment, perhaps? When you were little and someone said this to you, the only response you could ever think of would be to repeat those four words in a stupid voice, and maybe do a little dance of anger. Now that you are all grown up, you can handle it the adult way by using the two word response, the second of the two words would be either "you" or "off." So handle this unfeeling, flippant remark with the mature response it deserves. Then turn around, don't look back and slam the door on your way out.

"Happiness is just a state of mind."

Not profound. You could say that every emotion is just a state of mind: Happiness, sadness; deviousness; kindness. In fact, all of those words that end in *ness*. Does hearing that help? Do you want to hear someone stating the damn obvious? It's one of those sayings that a philosophy class could spend a whole semester analyzing and then write a thesis on. What does it mean? It means that it's an emotion and it can come and go. But so did our ex, and that's why we're in the state we are now in. Tell those helpful people to mind their own minds.

"Pull yourself together!"

Do well-intentioned people really think all your troubles will go away just because they reprimand you? I suppose kicking someone when they are down is their idea of making you feel better and helping you recover from this bad thing in your life. "Of course!" you say to them, "I never believed that pulling myself together would work, but if you suggest it, then it must be the cure for what I have. Can you tell me which pieces of me have come apart, so I can pull them back together again?" And don't forget the sarcastic smile.

PART FOUR

PICKING UP THE PIECES

A Snifter of Exorcism, Responsibility and Time Travel

Staying in Your Ex's Life

Accepting their new lover, or, a ménage a *quoi*?

*A*fter a relationship dies there's usually an injured party, someone who was hurt and left behind for dead. Let's say you are that person. Can you become friends with your ex, after the love has gone? Would you be able to move from a full, loving relationship to having a cup of coffee together with them once a week? As they finish their friendship coffee with you, they might say, "That was fun. Let's do it again next week. I'm going back to my apartment now, where my new girlfriend/boyfriend is waiting for me, while you continue your desolate, wretched life without me."

Now that's a good friendship!

The Tale of Alice

Keith and Alice lived together for nine years, and when Keith met someone else, he was sorry to have to tell Alice it was over because he thought she was a good person, and she "never done him no wrong." He let her know that he always wanted to be friends with her, but she loved him too much to be just friends and she had to break all ties with him. She took all of the photographs she had of them together out of her old-fashioned photo album, and reinserted them blank side up, so that they couldn't see how sad she was.

A few months later she was thinking about him while shopping at his end of town and decided to call him up to see how he was doing. He sounded happy to hear from her and invited her over for coffee. She gladly accepted—it would be really good to see him, she thought. A little like old times, only sad and perhaps poignant, but there would be coffee and that would be good.

When Keith opened the door he was beaming. "It's so great to see you!" he said truthfully, hugging her and bringing her in. "Come and sit down. The coffee's all ready." They chatted like the old friends they almost were and she was proud that she was able to keep her emotions under control, because deep down she was still not over him. When the coffee and the conversation had been enjoyed and then finished, she said she would have to leave. At the same time, the door to the master bedroom opened, cutting off their goodbyes as quickly as a guillotine to the head. Turning around in her seat, Alice saw an attractive young female emerge. She was pouty and lean, and was wearing nothing but one of Keith's shirts, accessorized by a post-coital smile. Alice knew instantly who it was—it was Replacement Alice, Keith's new girlfriend who had slid effortlessly into his life after she, Original Alice had been cast out. So, she really did exist and here she was in the flesh and certainly showing plenty of it.

When Replacement Alice saw Original Alice sitting with Keith, she stopped in her tracks and the post-sex smile faded away into a clot of embarrassment. Clutching Keith's shirt around her as if it were the last life vest on the Titanic, she shamefacedly wandered back into the bedroom, glancing over her shoulder at the couple sitting on the couch before she closed the door quietly behind her. Keith, meanwhile, was squirming in his seat like a small dog trying to shrug off a winter coat. "I'm so sorry," he said to Original Alice. "I wanted to see you, but Replacement Alice was here, so I asked her to hide in the bedroom until you left. I didn't want you to feel uncomfortable." Original Alice was lost for words. The man never ceased to amaze her. True to form, he then he amazed her again as he came up with yet another brilliant idea. "Hey!" he said. "I've got a brilliant idea! Wouldn't it be great if you and Replacement Alice could become friends? You really are very alike and you could hang out and have fun together."

"Fun" was a word that had been missing from Original Alice's vocabulary since Keith dumped her, and the thought of spending time with her replacement, who was sleeping with her boyfriend, was not really her idea of fun. Even if he did think they would have a lot in common. Perhaps Keith thought they could exchange tips on how to please him. Eventually they could become sister wives. Or better still, just slaves to him. The possibilities were endless. "Then we could all be friends together!" finished Keith, looking at Original Alice for approval.

"Tune in to next week's exciting episode. Can the two Alices become friends? Will they become mall buddies? Could Keith bring about world peace with his negotiating skills or will he start world war three in suburbia? Don't miss next week's episode: Alice Get Your Gun!"

Comment

It's difficult trying to be friends with someone you once shared everything with, including all of the love that God gave you. Your ex's world is changing and shifting away from you, so where is your niche in their world? Is there a place for you to be a friend of theirs alone, or is the only slot available one that includes their new partner? Or will you never be friends?

Comparing a committed relationship to a friendship is similar to likening a fast-moving speedboat ride to sitting on the side of the river. Riding on a speedboat is like a real relationship. It makes you feel intense, gives you emotions of pleasure, apprehension and happiness. A friendship touches more lightly on the emotions, is often more low-key, and the good feelings are less intense. It's calm and even, like the river as it flows by. So there you are, sitting on the riverbank as the speedboat of your relationship zooms past, with your ex on board. You give it a final wave goodbye as it races off to places of excitement and deep passions, leaving you to feed the ducks. "More bread?"

"Quack quack."

Can you remain friends with your ex? It's the type of decision that sometimes has to be tried, rather than decided by rational thinking. It's something that either falls into place or just falls flat on its face. Most of the time a friendship of exes follows a waiting period, like being at the doctor's or getting a license for a gun, the only difference is no one tells you when you're ready to reacquaint with your ex again. Original Alice may never be ready for a friendship with Keith and Replacement Alice. Perhaps she could find a Replacement Keith? That way Original Keith could have a sports buddy to watch the games with.

Letting Go of your Partner
Taking the Ted out of haunted

an you let go of your ex-partner emotionally after the break? Are you hanging on to the way of life that you had with them? Speculating if they are watching football or tennis? Wondering if they are cooking their spaghetti with white or red wine sauce this time? Is their memory haunting you and are you allowing it into your home, to sit with you on the couch or watch you in the shower? If so, it's part of not letting them go.

The Tale of Vanessa

It was a cold and dreary night. The wind was rapping on the door like an unwelcome salesman who had forgotten his samples in a stranger's living room. The rain fell light and rhythmically, releasing generous drops on and around the home, like wet flakes in a snow globe. An eerie whistling was heard; the sound of the wind letting itself in, uninvited through the windows, trying to attract the attention of Vanessa who was sitting on the couch. As she sat, she was aware of a ghostly presence in her home, but she was ignoring it, because Halloween was still two months away. She was watching Ted's favorite detective program on the TV and she suddenly solved the crime of "Who done It?" Turning to Ted, she exclaimed, "It was the realtor's wife!" But Ted had left her three weeks ago and with his detective-solving skills at a minimum, he wouldn't know who'd done it until he watched the following week's episode.

In her excitement at solving the mystery, Nessa had temporarily forgotten that Ted had moved out. She was used to having him around almost all of the time, but now her way of life had been split down the middle, like a corpse on the autopsy table. The tether of Ted's companionship had been cut. All that was left of him in their ex-marital apartment was some ectoplasm floating around in the attic and a coffee stain on the good tablecloth. Yet he was living in her mind like a phantom squatter.

Ted was the furthest thing from her mind as she drove to the bank the next day, humming his favorite song. Making a left turn on Leni Street, she happened to glance down at the steering wheel and noticed she was wearing her wedding ring. "That's very strange," she said to herself. Strange indeed, as she had removed it three weeks ago and put it away in a drawer when Ted had left. Could the ghost of Ted have gone into that drawer, taken out the ring and slipped it onto her finger when she wasn't looking? It couldn't be possible. It wasn't as though she had subconsciously done it herself. Or had she…?

The following afternoon, while hanging her clean laundry in the closet and reminding herself that Ted always liked the color green, she noticed a most peculiar thing. Her clothes were no longer spread out on the rack, but were all bunched up together on one side. She stopped what she was doing and stared, chewing thoughtfully on Ted's favorite gum. "What's going on?" she asked out loud. Why was Ted's side of the closet suddenly left open for him? His clothes were no longer there because he had taken them all, and up until then she had been utilizing that space for her own clothes. But now all of her things were back at her end again. She peered into the closet and half-expected to see something hiding in there, perhaps a squat, squeaking gremlin or a specter with an armload of clothes. "Nothing!" she said, closing the door.

Some heavy thinking followed while she made herself a cup of Ted's much-loved flavored coffee and that was when she decided that a poltergeist must be living in the apartment. That's why things kept being moved around. Or was she unwittingly making sure there was always room for Ted and his belongings? Fueled by her doubts and the newness of being alone still scratching at her skin, the hauntings continued.

Later on that week, while wearing an old t-shirt of Ted's she had found under the bed and working on a crossword puzzle of his from August, she was suddenly aware of the smell of his cologne. The scent caused her to write *tedcover* on the puzzle, instead of *bedcover,* and as she paused, pen in hand, she sniffed the air as a beagle would if it were on the scent of a small rodent, only in a more feminine way. Where was it coming from? As quickly as it came, it disappeared, as if the air had sucked it away. Had she really smelled it or was she mistaken? It wasn't as though she were still thinking about Ted, she reasoned. In fact, she believed she hardly thought about him at all.

Unable to come to terms with the strange events around the place, she called her mother. As a voice on the other end of the phone said, "Hello," she felt an icy finger drawing a circle on her back, then poking it in the center with cold, hard doubt. She pushed it away, but it was only her imagination giving her chills.

"Hello?" said Ted again. She pulled herself together.

"What are you doing at my mother's house?" she asked him, nervously tugging at her hair. There was a pause.

"Ted?"

"I'm not at your mother's house," he responded slowly, wondering if she had been dipping into the cooking sherry. "I'm at home. You must have dialed my home number by mistake." It suddenly hit her. Her whole body was being controlled by an outside force, and its name was Habit. Ted was gone, but she was so used to being around him, that she kept forgetting they weren't together anymore. At one time he lived in her home, but now he only lived in her head. And he wouldn't leave. She couldn't stop thinking about him and she hadn't even realized it.

Allowed the run of the home, the ghost of Ted continued to lurk in every room. It was in the CD player when she often found herself listening to his music and wondering why she didn't play something she liked. It slept in her toaster where she burnt her toast these days, just the way Ted liked it. It was in the jar of peanut butter where the accidental jelly hid inside, red eyes looking out at her and mocking her, because she never spilled jelly into the peanut butter, but Ted always did. Desperate actions needed to be taken and his ghost had to be removed from their once-shared home. Should she hire an exorcist to purge the ghost or should she take gingko, to improve her memory, and to remind her that Ted had moved out? Hmmm, exorcism or herbs? It was a close call.

But why was she still being haunted by Ted? It was true he was still in her head and yes, in her heart. But whatever the reason, it had to stop. Maybe Ted was haunting her because the apartment had so many memories of him.

Wherever she looked, she imagined she caught glimpses of him. He was sitting in the armchair with his coffee on the end table, and his imaginary slippers were under the couch. What could be done to remove these recollections? Perhaps she should move somewhere else, but she couldn't afford to do that. Maybe an overhaul of the décor would help distract her. If it looked different from when Ted lived there, the visions of him sitting here and resting there would be gone. If the couch was moved she wouldn't imagine his newspaper there, turned to the crossword puzzle page. If the table replaced the armchair, she couldn't picture him sitting in the chair. It would be a transformation for both the body and the mind. The task at hand was to make some drastic changes to the layout of her home and just like the new sheriff in town, she was the one to make them.

Tedless Feng Shui became a priority and Nessa decided to make the rooms look different by moving the furniture around. The tall lamp and high-backed chair did a two-step with the couch and they traded places. The table resentfully switched its corner with the armchair. It didn't quite fit into the smaller space and you could tell it wasn't happy there, standing at a bit of an angle. But once everything was done, it looked very different, almost like someone else's home.

It took a little while for Nessa to be reminded that Ted was gone and it was achieved by a sequential number of stages. Step 1: She still forgetfully called out from the kitchen to ask him what he wanted to eat. Of course there was always no answer. Not unusual anymore. Step 2: She walked from the kitchen into the living room to look for him. Step 3: She would get whacked on the kneecap by the ever-vengeful table. Step 4: While rubbing her kneecap she remembered

Ted wasn't there anymore. By week two, she was limping from cuts and bruises on her knees, shins and ankles, but she was smiling because Ted's ghost seemed to be fading.

The next task was to exorcise the ghost completely and she burned, hid, discarded or unplugged anything that reminded her of Ted. Along with changing the way her home looked, she also changed her appearance from a matronly Nessa to a sexy and bruised Nessa. Now the transformation of her single life was complete. Ted's ghost had been exorcised by changing Nessa's surroundings, helped along with a little gingko. Nessa was no longer possessed by a ghost.

Comment

It's possible that these types of home hauntings were the inspiration for Hollywood moviemakers, giving them the notion for horror films. They used chilling music to give it greater impact and if you want to encourage the haunting memory of your ex, you too could add music. Classical piano or harpsichord is usually the best, or something religious.

Eliminating memories can put you on the road to healing. It's difficult to wipe them out of your mind, but making visual changes can remove the ones you see all around you. The memory of your ex might be wrapped around your mind like mating vipers and equally as dangerous, but often you need to make a determined effort to exterminate them. Once the thoughts of your ex and the habit of them is broken, you may say to yourself with a sigh of relief, "Aaaaaah. Thank goodness this won't end with a dead bat in the attic and drops of ram's blood on the new beige carpet. It's so hard to get blood out of beige. I was freed just in the nick of time!"

Single and Out of Control
Let's jump on the casual sex bandwagon

S ome people marry their first love and may never have had sex with more than one person in their entire lives. When their relationship ends, they may have a jones for some casual sex with different partners. Back in the olden days it was called sowing your wild oats, but these days it's more commonly known as getting lucky, and often goes along with an elbow nudge and a wink.

The Tale of Jack

Jack married young and when his wife Shelly left him eight years later, it was the opening of the casual sex floodgates. His looks had held up pretty well and his conversation became more outgoing as time went on, but it was his manner that netted him the women. He spoke very softly so that the women had to move in close enough to feel his breath on their cheek in order to hear him, and he had a way of looking at a lady so intently that it made her feel like the only woman on earth.

His friends were in awe of this casual-sex maestro and talked admiringly about him behind his back and also to his face, but their wives and girlfriends didn't approve of him, thinking he would lead their husbands astray. They would interrogate their husbands with, "Are you meeting That Jack tonight?" And Jack's reputation gained such heights that he was no longer just simply "Jack," but had grown to become "That Jack. The Jack of all Jacks. A Jack to be respected."

At the suggestion of their women, the guys mentioned to Jack that they were concerned about him.

"Cool it," they told him. "You don't know anything about some of these women you are taking home."

But his response was always, "You know why I do this. I need to catch up on the dating I missed out on before I was married. How can I say no to them?" He thought his friends were jealous because he rarely went home alone, and he was right. But he thrilled them with his escapades, wowed them with his ploys, astounded them with tales of his positions, and he was the most popular guy on the south side of town.

Friday night was happy hour at The Crowded Abyss, a blue-collar hangout on the corner of N. Main and Walter Street. Even though Jack went to bars and clubs most nights, he rarely drank, but on August 16th, Jack was having a birthday, and his friends and the Walter Street Girls insisted on buying him drinks all night. These girls worked in the margarine factory across the street and were known for their slick ways. The laughs and the flirting went on until the early hours of the morning until Jack hailed himself a taxi home. He didn't remember anything after that, and also some events before that, including when Lynette followed him into the men's room at around 1 a.m. to bring him a drink.

Saturday morning brought offensive bright sunshine and a headache sandwich to Jack. As he lay in bed trying to assemble his thoughts out of random order and into some sense, he noticed an unpleasant smell of putrid sweat and sour alcohol. He did the blow-sniff check, where you cup your hand to your mouth, breathe out then sniff quickly to smell your breath. Pretty bad, but not that bad. Suddenly, the silence of the room was shattered by a snort, reminiscent of a wild boar in heat. His heart pounded in his chest and his headache disappeared for a few seconds while his mind tried to figure out what was going on. His brain went into search mode, rapidly scanning every sound he had ever heard in his past, trying to make a comparison to the snort that shook his bed so that he would know what it was. The search halted at a memory from the petting zoo when he was six years old, when the momma pig had snorted at him when he tried to pick up one of her piglets.

He was pretty sure there were no sows or piglets in his room, but he was still afraid to look around. Another snort shook the bed. Someone was laying next him. He braced himself and reluctantly turned his head. It wasn't a sow, but it might have been her cousin, the pig-lady. There she lay, fast asleep, naked and with breasts reclining comfortably under her flaccid arms. As she snored, the spiky black hairs on her top lip quivered and her nose whistled a thin, three-note melody. The old booze came back up into his throat and then went back down again and he coughed a little, waking up this creature from the black lagoon.

Maybe God didn't owe him any favors, but he prayed to Him anyway. He prayed the prayer of the remorseful drunk: "Please tell me I didn't. Dear God, please tell me I didn't…" The slumbering creature stretched, and then reached out to him. The word that melted cheese-like from her lips filled him with horror. "More."

Comment

People binge on sex for a multitude of reasons and some binge for no reason. After a partner leaves, some people feel that sex with multiple partners expresses their freedom and they enjoy it. Others may be angry at their ex for the break up, and use willing strangers in an almost abusive way for misdirected revenge to sate their anger. Lonely people take comfort in the intimacy that a warm body can offer. Several people just like to have sex and simply want to jump the guy on the bus. At the time, alcohol temporarily gives us permission to have casual sex without guilt, but if the stone-cold sobriety of the next morning causes us to look around and say, "Oh no, it's you!" just remember, it's not love, and you can quit cold turkey.

Going it alone
Confronting the daytime terrors of State Government

When unpleasant tasks need to be done, or when confrontational situations occur, it's good to have someone to come home to. It means everything to have a shoulder to cry on, a sympathetic person to reassure us, or a friendly ear to relate a story to. It's often physically or psychologically more difficult to cope with a situation when you are one-strong. But you are not alone in your aloneness. Think of all of the other single people in the world being a family of strangers together. They could always be there for you when you need comfort. Let's call them the family of Singlers.

The Tale of Casey

Casey coped reasonably well after Monica went her own way because he was always a strong, independent man. He never quite managed to go to the supermarket, but he shopped at the local convenience store for his meals, paid his bills on time, made it into work every day and even enjoyed a sparse social life. But Casey had a fear of the Department of Motor Vehicles. In the past, Monica was his DMV rock, and she gave him encouragement when he had to renew his driver's license or car registration, or pick up new license plates. She would be there waiting for him when he returned home, with the primeval stench of sweat about him that signified fight or flight. During the honeymoon phase of their relationship, where you can't seem to do enough for each other and familiarity hasn't tainted you, she would go along with him for support.

But now he was facing that many-headed demon alone and he knew how Hercules felt when he had to conquer the Hydra. Casey's driver's license expiration date was noted in black marker on his calendar from James Bacco Insurance, Inc., highlighted in yellow, the color of sweat and circled in red, the color of blood. As the day before the expiration grew closer, Casey became more restless. He began fighting with people at work; he ate less and slept only sporadically. The day finally came: Friday June 13th.

DMV fever set in hard that day. He had a temperature of 99.8 degrees and a magenta rash of rebellion had settled over his chest and on the back of his hands. He carried the stare of a methamphetamine junkie in his eyes. He stepped into his car and drove like a man hypnotized by a Las Vegas showman, parked his car at the DMV and went in.

Step One: "Where do I park when I get there?" had been conquered, and he didn't even need to think about it.

Step Two was the most difficult of all: "Which line do I stand in?" If he knew in his mind that he had someone to come home to, someone who would tell him, "It's all over now. Hush, hush," he would feel comforted in his search for the right line to wait in. Unfortunately, he no longer had such a person. But Casey knew about the family of Singlers and he drew his strength from them, knowing that they too had visited the DMV at some time, and had done it alone. He was directed to a specific line to stand in by an information specialist, and after waiting 15 minutes in that line, there was a discrepancy and suddenly it was the wrong line. This was the horror of the optional Step Three.

Optional Step Three was the one of his nightmares: "What if I'm in the wrong line?" As the nausea rose in his gut Casey said to himself, "As a single person I am not alone. Other people who are alone do difficult things like this every day. They make me strong." It was this thought that stopped him from running back to his car. After only a fifteen minute wait, it was his turn. The paperwork wasn't quite right, but the kindly man helped with that. It may have been because of the numbness of death he saw when he looked into Casey's eyes, but the man went out of his way to help. He even took more than one picture so that Casey could choose the best one. Hmmm, should he pick the one that made him look like he needed a blood transfusion or the one that made him look like a simpleton who had run amok with a pitchfork? Finally, he let the man decide.

Once home, he made himself comfortable in his favorite chair, opened a bottle of tequila and drank a toast to himself, a man not alone in a world of aloneness. Casey had gained strength from knowing that there are people out there who are terrified of doing things all by themselves and he was one of them. He was a soldier in the vast army of Singlers. A man with a family of human beings unknown to him, but who he knew would understand his fears. The Singlers were just like him.

Comment

We are all obligated to do things we hate to do, and things that make us fearful, but we must appreciate that others have these fears too. Knowing that fact can make all the difference in the world and give us the strength we need to face and conquer our problems alone. The Family of Singlers sympathizes with all of your troubles, and the only reason they are not physically there for you is because they don't know you. They could be your biggest fans, your best encouragement, and your comfort at the DMV, immigration or the unemployment line. There are millions of Singlers who return to empty homes at the end of the day, just like you, and they know how you feel. They have been in your situation and are rooting for you. We are only human after all, and we all live with our own fears. But, if you need a friend, call up the Family of Singlers in your mind. Think of them as your holiday pals at Christmas, helping you to pick out that tree, or the buddy you call when your workday falls apart, and whenever you raise your glass, drink a toast to them!

When the Subconscious Selects a Date

Familiarity breeds repetition

*I*t's hard to get back into the dating mode when you really don't want anyone else except your lost love. You know that no one will measure up to them. Even if you managed to get your hands on the best looking, most interesting perfect person, they still wouldn't measure up to that cross-eyed, snaggle-toothed, semi-illiterate person who threw you out of the house into the snow on your birthday. You are used to that person. You still love that person. Why would you want to date anyone else?

The Tale of Dominic

It took Dominic only a couple of months to be ready for dating again after his split with Megan. He always gravitated to the same type of woman—petite, dark eyed, dark-haired and cuddly, but that type of woman was oil to his water and the match never seemed to mix properly, no matter how much it was shaken up, and Megan had been no exception. She was a lady who liked the men too much, just like the other girlfriends he had chosen and he felt a drastic change would only do him good. His ideal woman was going to be the Anti-Megan: slim, blonde, and tall, rather like Ken's Barbie. After all, he was tall and blond like Ken, so they would make the ideal couple.

To find the perfect love, he searched bar and club, park and gym and met many svelte, fair-haired women, but they were all lacking. If they were blonde, they weren't tall; if they happened to be tall, they were too cuddly, like Megan, and if they were tall and blond, they had dark eyes. When he met Skyler in a bar at 2 a.m. one Saturday, he knew she wasn't what he was looking for, and her smile was more "lose some" than winsome, but he was inexplicably attracted to her. He blamed it on the martinis and asked to see her again, and she said yes. When they spoke on the phone the next day, he asked her out to dinner for the following Friday night. They arranged to meet inside rather than outside of La Petite Portion Restaurant, as it was February and a chill wind was blowing through everyone that particular week, because it was too lazy to blow around them.

Dominic arrived early at the restaurant and stood by the entranceway, his eyes adjusting to the dark ambience produced by the red velvet lamps on the walls that the restaurant had imported from Paris, but were made in China anyway. Once his vision had adjusted to the dim lighting he gazed around the room looking for Skyler. A familiar face caught his eye. It couldn't be! But it was! It was Megan, his old flame. He immediately saw that she looked great and his heart skipped a beat. And then it skipped another because she was all alone. Then it started pounding. Should he go over and talk to her? Surely there was no harm in doing that, and she did look good. In fact, he had never seen her in that red dress before because she always wore pants. He cautiously walked in the direction of her table, keeping one eye on the door watching for Skyler. When Megan caught sight of him, her face lit up and she smiled and beckoned him over. There was no mistaking that look; she was still really attracted to him.

He hurried over to her table. Maybe she would want to get back together again? As she stood up to greet him, all earthly logic disappeared and he felt like he was floating in space because everything seemed to be moving in slow motion, like film footage of astronauts. He felt his perception of time lagging behind real time and he couldn't catch up with what was going on. His brain was trying to put together what he saw, but seemed unable to do so. Megan looked at him and said, "Hi," but it wasn't her. What was going on?

"Hi," he stammered as he tried to place the face before him.

"Good to see you," responded Skyler as she leaned in to kiss him. It wasn't Megan after all. It was Skyler, and boy did she look like Megan. He had made a rookie re-dating mistake. He was Twin Dating.

Comment

Twin Dating is when you date people who look like or who remind you of your ex. We may not realize it, but it's reassuring to date someone who reminds us in a good way of a person who we are already familiar with. We may say about those people, "I've only known them for an hour, but it feels like I've know them all of my life." Have you ever smiled at a stranger who reminded you of your Uncle Clark and been a little surprised when they didn't smile back? Doesn't it make you wonder if you were on this earth before? Reincarnation theories aside, if we make a decision to change the type of person we have been associating with, it's often hard or even impossible to do.

That's why actors date actors and rich folk date rich folk. It seems to work when we keep our lifestyles familiar to what we already know. When we cross that "different" line and date the type of person we are not used to being around, it can feel awkward. It might be exciting at first, but after a while we crawl back to our roots. Stay in your comfort zone, but don't go to extremes like Dom. Twin Dating can become quite boring after a while and make you feel like you are dating the same person every time. There's only one thing that's worse than Twin Dating and that's Self-Dating. That's when you only date people who look like you. But that one is a little more creepy and narcissistic and hopefully not relevant here.

Time Travel
Going back 10 years to find where I left myself

Doom comes in many forms. It precedes gloom and despondency. It rides on the back of the grim reaper. It appears on dark nights in a haunted house high up on a hill where teenagers are screaming and wearing ripped shirts, and sometimes it comes at the cusp of a breakup, as it did for Sally.

During most relationships, you are invited to live in your partner's world with their family and friends. You don't need to respond to this kind of an invitation, you just show up and everyone welcomes you, except maybe for their jealous cousin, who has had a crush on Cousin Nick for the last

15 years. You, in turn, will invite them into your world. It's almost like a dance. In a perfect world you would spend half of your time with their family and friends and half with yours. But a perfect 50/50 balance exists only with a court-mandated order and luckily, most relationships don't have those.

People who are drawn into spending 90 percent of their time in their partner's world and only 10 percent in their own, sometimes begin to resemble their better halves, but luckily not in the same way that some dog owners begin to look like their dogs. Sadly, people who live too close to someone else can easily become an opposite-sex version of their significant other, and it has nothing to do with either steroids or hormones. Their partner's habits and idiosyncrasies begin to rub off on them like cheap gold plating and they may too-readily call their lover's father "Big Daddy," and the mother, "Sugar." It's not healthy to move into someone else's world and become a clone of them, leaving your own friends and relatives behind. Because then, if your partner drops you like the proverbial hot potato, you have to untangle yourself from their world to unearth the original you. Only when you have dug yourself out of that hole and shaken off all of the dirt and small insects, can you be yourself again.

The Tale of Sally

Sally was a little butterball of a young woman. She had a colorful persona, a little shy and firm around the corners and more soft on the inside, like a croissant. Nick, her boy-friend, was attracted to her artistic and original way of look-ing at things, especially the photographs she took of garden gnomes and the songs she wrote about heartache and head-ache. He possessed a much stronger personality than Sally and was more outgoing than she was, and she liked that in a man. He was an expert woodcarver and she was just a nov-ice whittler and that made for a good balance between them, with give on one side and take on the other.

But Sally was a girl without heartache insurance because she allowed her personality to morph into his. This meant that after she moved herself and her personality into his world, abandoning her own, any heartache resulting from a breakup would be as fat as a Thanksgiving turkey and just as doomed. Regrettably, her doom lurked just down the road from year three.

Sally's life with Nick was more like Nick's life with Sally in it. Her smaller personality was lost in the tall grasses of Nick's existence, like a bastard field mouse, and she no longer had a life of her own. It didn't seem like she had sold her soul to the devil, but maybe the devil wouldn't have agreed with that. To Sally, everything had become easier because most of the decisions in her life were now being made by Nick and she willingly went along with them. All she had to do was get up in the morning and follow orders. It was similar to being in the armed forces, but without the marching and the ugly camouflage clothing.

Nick didn't like her friends very much, and one by one he encouraged her to let them go. At first Sally missed Susan and Pauline, especially their monthly ice cream sun-dae eating contests and the new diets they began the fol-lowing day. After a while she didn't really miss Soap Opera Saturdays and Fingernail Appliqué Sundays with Cassi and Torri, and too quickly her friends were just a distant memory, like a boat in the Bermuda Triangle. When Sally tried to cajole Nick into seeing her family from time to time, Nick would think up something for them both to do that was much more fun, like whitewater rafting, dog racing or brunch at the Elite Hotel, that not even her grandmother Judy could afford.

Sally enjoyed living Nick's life. It was so much more fun than her life had been pre-Nick, when she lived alone in a one-room apartment and when her menu consisted of canned soup and cereal. Her social life with her friends wasn't exciting back then, and the visits from her boring family and their noisy children were just a prelude to an evening of washing dishes after they left, and spot-cleaning the carpet where little Pippa spilt her grape juice. *Kelly Does Zumba* on the TV was the kick-start to her Monday evenings, and there was nothing exciting in Sally's old life. But Nick's life was story-book fun and she had been invited to live inside the pages.

His family and friends lived in Alaska and both Nick and Sally wanted to visit them there. When Nick suggested they pack everything up and move to Alaska instead, Sally was thrilled. They rented a cabin on the edge of a cubic zirconia-sparkling lake where there were mountains all around and beautiful wild beasts lived nearby. At night they would listen to the howling of the wolves and make up stories about them. In the daytime they would hike together and she would take photographs of tiny flowers and pollinating insects, and Nick carved a table that they ate their food from. Their life together was digital-photograph perfect.

Nick's family and friends lived a few miles away from their log cabin, and Sally became very attached to his family, his friends, and those friends' girlfriends and children. The move into Nick's world was like walking over black ice that was hidden by a soft snowfall, and she fell right into it. They were both happy with the way things were and they danced together under the stars during the summer barbeques. It was fascinating to be in the center of someone else's life; almost as though she *were* that other person. At this point you might be saying, "Oh-oh. This doesn't sound good, at all." And you would be right. With Nick as her gatekeeper, he held the key to her life, which now had the feel of a 1970's acoustic folk song about happy people and good drugs, and women in long, brightly colored skirts wearing too many beads.

But thunder struck her little Ponderosa one day when Nick found himself another mountain maiden and suggested that Sally find a different cozy log cabin to live in. So what happens when the gatekeeper takes the key from your world and subsequently stops you from entering a place you enjoyed visiting? What happens if the key that unlocked the only life you have known for years is suddenly taken away, and that life is closed to you? You could try kicking in the lock, or pounding on the door, but even if someone does let you back in, no-one really wants to see you again.

When they broke up, Sally's life as she knew it was closed to her. Flung into a single and Nickless world where she didn't belong was devastating. And, after being "Nick's Sally" for so many years, her own world had been neglected and rusted away to a hollow shell, with nothing in it except for her lonely self. Her identity was no more and she was stranded between worlds.

Comment

Some time ago your ex-partner brought you into their world as a gift for being their other half and now they took that gift back, leaving you with nothing. You not only give up your ex's lifestyle when you break up, you also give up their friends. You may be forced to leave behind a whole world of people that your ex introduced you to, who may have become more of a part of your life than your original friends.

After being banished from your story-book world, you may not even want to be the old you anymore. The new you was more fun, had more money and many more friends, but really it wasn't you. You were just borrowing the persona of your ex. Perhaps they selfishly turned you into the person that they needed, and now you are not allowed to be that person anymore, but Oh my God! You have forgotten what it is like to be you. Look at yourself now, how did you become that chain-smoking, fast talking, bleached blonde hillbilly with the cosmetic dental work? You don't resemble yourself at all anymore! However, you are in there somewhere and someone is bound to remember you. Look at old photographs of yourself which might give you a clue as to what you liked to do and how you liked to dress. Once you are familiar with your original self again, indulge yourself a little and be very kind to you, because if you are unkind, you just might find yourself taking off again into someone else's world. And then where would you be?

Your own world will always be there for you to clamber back into. The walls might be a little shaky and the neighbors might have moved on and there's probably a big spider web in the corner, but wipe off the dust from the folding chair, sit down and call everyone you once knew because now you have some good stories to tell them. And if they used to be your friends and family back in The Day, they still will be now, and will most likely find it in their hearts to take you back. Oh, and buy some decent furniture, that old stuff is so outdated.

Listening to Music
Unbreaking your heart through song

id you ever take a small animal to the veterinarian in a closed box with breathing holes punched into the sides? Once you open that lid, you don't know what the reaction of the little beast will be. Will it be anger, tranquility or an instinct to fight with tooth and claw? Picture yourself as a cat that is going to the vet's to get fixed. When the lid opens, what does your feline mind think will happen? Answer: you don't quite know. It's very much how we feel when we are riding the elevator and a terrible version of *This Will Always Be Our Song, Baby*, suddenly warbles through the ceiling vent. Do we wipe away the tears, or punch a hole in the elevator door, trying to get out? Music can take us by surprise because it's just as emotional as a trip to the vet.

It builds memories when we first hear it, then it brings back memories when we hear it again. We express ourselves through music and in turn, it affects our moods. Once a relationship is over, listening to certain songs or compositions can cause us to have specific emotional reactions, and even if we have been holding our emotions in check extremely well, that snippet of a song can knock us off our feet and into the doldrums of despair. But music can be beneficial; it can help us determine our mood, heal us, or get us over the hump of sadness or anger we feel at the moment. If all music came with a mood warning, just like medications come with alerts of possible side effects, we could prevent ourselves from inadvertently listening to the wrong kind. Equally, listening to the right kind of music could enhance a good mood that we didn't think we could conjure up.

The Tale of Zandrea

The scene is sometime in the future. Everyone's name begins with a Z like it used to do in those really old sci-fi B movies. It could be real life, a cartoon, or maybe it *is* one of those old B movies. Zandrea is wandering around the music store. She is feeling numb after her separation from Zalex and wonders why she is unable to cry. What kind of music should she listen to that would make her shed tears, so that she could ultimately feel better? She wanders over to the Jazz section and looks at the mood descriptions and alerts on some of the soulful jazz and ballad CDs. She reads: "Warning. Can cause tearing of the eyes and soulful sobbing." That seems to be how she might want to feel, given the circumstances, and she picks out a couple of CDs.

Wandering over to the Country and Western section she reads the alerts on some of those CDs: "Warning. Can increase thoughts of depression and despondency."

"Well, that's more like it," she thinks. "I should be feeling pretty despondent right about now." So she chooses some particularly sad songs with titles such as "My Baby

Got Run Over By the 12:50 From Memphis," and "Gotta Cry, Wanna Die, Can't Dance No More," and she just had to buy the "My Kid's Momma's Done Gone and Left Me for a Rodeo Clown" CD which included other semi-suicidal compilations.

Cut to the main entrance, where Zadam walks into the store. He knows he feels angry and wants to listen to some music that will feed the demons in his soul. Arrogantly walking over to the punk section, he reads the alert on a CD that features a blood-covered skull in the cover art: "Warning. May instigate violence." Perfect. He selects a few more punk CDs and then strolls over to the rap section. "Warning. May cause disrespect, later followed by dancing." He knew then that the perfect evening lay ahead, and it would be a night to be remembered.

Comment

An added bonus could be that you might meet people in a particular section who feel the same way you do and you could commiserate together. But until music with a mood warning on the label comes to a store near you, you may want to avoid you and your ex's song, "I Love You More Than The Lottery," or music from a pre-breakup concert, or anything that elicits memories of you and your ex. So at the moment, the only warning carried on music is "Parental advisory—explicit content," and that may well describe the language you used the day of the breakup. But other warnings might be on the way in The Future, because music is a powerful mood enhancer. It can lift you up to your zenith, make you zone out like a zombie or just make you over-zealous like a zany zebu that drank too much zythum.

Sleeping Alone

Closing your eyes to an empty bed

How much are you aware of while you are sleeping? Pretty much only your dreams. It might give you comfort to know that someone is lying next to you while you sleep, but it is estimated that people sleep 65% better when sleeping alone. Who wants to listen to snoring and nose whistling, or be kicked and have the covers stolen from your icy feet by their icy feet? You're better off sleeping solo, look how rested you'll be the next day, your face will show 65% of relaxation down one side, plus you'll impress everyone you know when they say, "Hey, why have you got that big grin on your face? It must have been a good night!"

"Yes," you respond, "It was. All nine hours of it."

"Wow. Nine hours. I wish I was single again."

You see, just by being single, you can impress people. Relationships are so overrated.

The Tale of Miriam

Peter and Miriam were like most couples and slept together in the same bed, but Miriam had always resented Peter's nighttime behavior, which worsened as the years went by.

It wasn't only the snoring or the odd smells. Nor was it just the tossing and turning and monopolizing of all of the covers that irritated Miriam and disrupted her sleep. It was his timing and somnambulistic aggression. He had a recurring dream that he was in the army.

Peter's sleeping body rarely rested. In the middle of the night it would come to life as he dreamed. He mostly dreamt that he was a soldier and many evenings were a battle for both Peter and Miriam. In the morning neither of them would wake up rested. At around 1 a.m. Peter's dream would begin with reveille, followed by inspection. Miriam was, of course, asleep at this point and it wasn't until the General made his appearance that Peter inadvertently woke her. His arm would rise up quickly from the pillow in salute and on the way up, his elbow would always catch some sensitive part of her body, and on its way back down, his hand would graze her face and she would swat it away as if it were some giant housefly.

By then she was wide awake, but because the inspection itself was something of a quiet time for them both, Miriam was able to fall back to sleep for quite a while. Then the marching would start and like a dreaming dog chasing a cat, Peter's arms and legs would start to twitch and Miriam would wake up again. Because the marching was fairly rhythmic, she would find herself dozing along to the regular beat of the twitches, but if the troops were singing cadence, she was out of luck, as Peter would begin to sing along.

Peter had explained the recurring dream to Miriam and she suggested, no, begged him to ask his doctor for something to help him relax him at night, but he refused. As he was unable to join the regular army because of his bad knees, bedtime was only time when he could be a soldier, and every night he dutifully marched with the Somnambulist Army.

It was lucky for Miriam that Peter's nighttime army never went to war while they were together. She shivered at the thought of Peter loading a rifle and shooting the enemy. *Boom*! She would be the one with the injuries the next morning. It was bad enough her erotic dreams of the UPS delivery guy in various forms of undress were disturbed night after night. Peter put an end to those fantasies with his army games faster than a movie director calling out, "Cut!" It was strange, because it was as if he knew she was playing around in her sleep and he saw fit to punish her. But now she slept alone and never looked back. Yes, sleeping alone has its own share of benefits.

Comment

Just because you are not fighting with the military in your sleep, doesn't mean you don't have your own battles in the bedroom. It's common to be kept awake by a partner who snores, while others bear the burden of sleeping with those clingy folk, the ones who try to sleep right on top of you like a mating locust. Also exhibiting insect behavior are the singing cricket sleepers, those who rub their feet together while trying to go to sleep. The hyper-active snoozers are up all night sleepwalking, sleeptalking or sleephumming, and like heavy drinkers of alcohol, they can't remember a thing in the morning.

Relationships, like battles, can be lost because of exhaustion and lack of sleep, because sleep is something that cannot be taken, it can only be given. That's why people say,

"I'm going to get some sleep," like they are trying to buy drugs. "Pssst! I need to get me some sleep. How much for a nighttime bag? Twenty bucks? Dude, I can get me some sleep cheaper than that downtown!"

But look at it this way, how can you miss someone if you are asleep? Of course, before you fall asleep, there is the pre-slumber bonding, snuggling, reading, and wild sex, and then it's "lights out," and time to sleep. The actual sleeping you do by yourself. What if you wake up after a nightmare and there's no one there for you, you ask? If you need to wake up with someone next to you after a nightmare, you are probably too young to be sleeping with someone anyway. You should be glad you are finally getting some rest. It's a pity you can't sell some of that good sleep to your married friends.

Pre-Dating

Am I cool, or am I just numb?

eing unsociable is cool. Friendships and relationships that take up your time are vastly overrated. Put on some sunglasses and it doesn't matter how angry, miserable or self-consumed you are. People will look at you and say, "See that guy over there in the shades? He's cool."

Only you alone will know that it's not true.

Once your relationship is over, there will come a time when you should close your eyes, hold your nose and your breath, then jump back into the socializing scene. Some will swim well and meet friendly people out there, but others will hit the diving board smack! in the center of their chin, curse silently to themselves and sport a bruise after they dry off. When your friends drag you out and you are kicking and screaming and rubbing the bruise on your chin, the opposite sex may not approach you in a bar—well, not until after several cocktails, anyway.

Staying home alone each night can be depressing and damagingly self-indulgent, and if your friends don't drag you out, you may be enticed into the night by a good movie, a new restaurant, a party, or the hunt for companionship or sex. Some stumble out only after the consumption of alcohol at home has made them more sociable. Others, like Richard in the story below, feel they have done enough of a comfortable solitary confinement, and they should now grant themselves a little parole away from the usual action-packed Saturday night spent dozing in front of the TV.

The Tale of Richard

Richard tried hard to be sociable after Julia left him. His socializing consisted of saying hello to his neighbors, chatting to his cat Benita as he cleaned out her litter box and interacting with the TV by answering questions out loud from game shows. Being sociable with real people hadn't yet crossed his mind because it was still full of Julia. His friends were a group of young guys who moved like the ball in a pinball machine, hitting on their conquests, making bells ring and lights flash, then rolling on by to the next lady. They weren't interested in relationships, just in having a good time. Richard was not one of their kind, but he was their friend, despite being a one-woman man. It took several weeks to persuade Richard to come out with them, but one night he switched off the television set and left the house with misgivings on his mind and Julia still riding high in his heart.

It was a lethargic and reluctant Richard that left his home that Saturday night to go out with his friends, but Richard's friends saw him as a new, detached Richard, who was unlike the friendly, chatty Richard of old, and they were impressed. This new Richard was cool. Ice cool. He wore his sunglasses all of the time, even in the dark clubs. Like a rock star. His behavior was also chilly to any lady who came along and showed an interest in him. At the first sentence of introduction, Richard swiveled around on his bar stool and turned his back on the poor girl until she left. This resulted in the victim running to the ladies' room in tears and asking her friends, "What's wrong with me? Am I so ugly that people can't bear to look at me, even in the dark? And he's wearing SUNGLASSES for goodness sake!" It was unusual behavior, especially for a man, but Richard's friends thought it was cool. They were impressed that he was playing hard to get by making the women beg for his cooler than cool attention. They were all in awe of this dude with the 24/7 night-time shades.

But Richard was not only cool on the outside. His whole self was frigid and his blood ran cold inside a freezing body. A doctor would have diagnosed him as having *Tristis Pectus Pectoris* (which translated from the Latin means a broken heart), and most likely would have recommended many nights out on the town, with a shot of whiskey for warmth and a cuddly lady to take out the chill. His illness was heart-ache. Nothing more. Poor Richard wasn't the "cool" dude his friends thought him to be. He was still getting over Julia. He was going through that numb stage that's normal right after a breakup, where you force yourself to go out thinking once you make that huge effort, you will have a good time. This numb period involves sitting in a bar or club, all dressed up like a Christmas mannequin in a New York store-front, but being too shell-shocked to talk to anyone of the opposite sex. He was frozen in the pre-healing phase and turning away was his only solution. The promise of good food, drinks, music and sexy girls wearing tiny dresses just didn't work for Richard. There was almost a hate inside him for all things female.

It was a long time before he was ready to date again and take that first step of smiling at a woman, because no-one could make him forget Julia. But by the time he did, he had earned the reputation of being "that cool dude with the shades who plays hard-to-get." Richard's sunglasses were a good touch to add that extra coolness to his image. They also hid eyes that were red-rimmed and swollen from crying over his lost love. The story of Richard has a happy ending for him. Several months later, when he went back out on the dating scene all healed and ready for action, the girls were waiting for him. It was easy pickins, like calling out the next number at the deli counter.

Comment

There is no time limit on this phase. Experiencing it and then emerging from it all depends on the personality of the hurt party. But you have to leave the womb of your home to recover, so take your aloneness and lock it in your living room. Prop it up in a comfortable chair in front of a movie with a cheap TV dinner and sneak out the back door. It'll still be there when you return home, and maybe you can even enjoy a bit of it when you get back, along with a side of peace and quiet. But at least you can pat yourself on the back for trying out the world that exists around you, instead of the world that has been living inside your head. And if you've been living inside your head for too long, you'll start to hear voices. And they won't be saying "go out."

Money Woes
Beating your bills into submission

veryone loves a scandal. It's number four on the list of things we enjoy the most, along with sex, chocolate, and a good book. Or maybe a warm brandy on a snowy night. Or a Chihuahua puppy on our lap. Or a phone call from a friend when we feel lonely. But still, everyone loves a scandal, because that's what makes life exciting, and if we aren't doing those scandalous things ourselves, we are content in knowing that other people are doing them. If they are bad scandals, where someone is suffering, we also enjoy them, because we are glad we are not the ones in pain. Yes, nature made us selfish, heartless and uncaring when it comes to scandals, and it also allowed us to judge others. And we love judging others. That's why God made reality TV and soap operas.

After a separation you may end up with half, or more than half of the joint assets, but it doesn't mean you can afford to pay your bills all by yourself. You may even think about hanging onto that partner you just can't stand anymore if he has a job. But if you are true to yourself and honest and decide to let them go, you may not only be feeling a loss in your heartstrings, but also your purse strings. The shared bills of old are now just the unpaid bills of new. But watch out for the gossips in the neighborhood, because if they catch of glimpse of their neighbor's money problems, they can cause that person's humiliation to ripen into a full-blown scandal.

The Tale of Francine

When Francine and Bryan divorced, the alimony and the child support payments disappeared out of state on a midnight train to Albuquerque, along with Bryan and his suitcase, never to be seen again. Even though money was tight when they were together, the bills were always paid on time, or minimum payments were met. Once alone, Fran was concerned because the money just wasn't there. But life had a way of moving on regardless and it always took her along with it. Although she struggled with the money issues, after a while she fell into a routine. Unfortunately, it was a routine of the worst possible kind, and after a while, Fran found herself building a skeleton out of her bad habits; and she hid that skeleton in her closet.

Fran harbored a dark secret of evasion that not even her family knew about, until that fateful Tuesday in May. She had lain awake the night before, the secret pressing so hard on her body that it was difficult for her to turn her head and she anxiously stole out of bed at 2 a.m. This was the time when everyone's drapes were closed and all but the dancers and shift workers were asleep. Leaving the door unlocked, she tiptoed out of the house without first getting dressed.

The full moon stared at her, turning its flattened nose up at her cheap nightdress and silently criticizing her. She pulled her robe tightly around her to hide the frayed hem. She walked to her mailbox and opened the door and stared at the accumulated mail of the financially deprived. She reached out to take it, but she couldn't touch it. It seemed to radiate a heat that repelled her hand, like a north-to-north magnet and she closed the door, her hand empty and sweating. It was a tragedy, but she couldn't deal with the contents of the envelopes. The red numbers and the angry threats would have to wait yet another week. If she didn't take the bills, she didn't have to pay the bills. Anyone could understand that. She went back into her bedroom and closed the door. Across the street at number 112, the drapes twitched and even at such a late hour, Mrs. Klatsch picked up her phone to call Mrs. Chismes at number 33. The scandal was unfolding.

It was the following day, and Fran's mother had stopped by in the afternoon to babysit while Fran went to the dentist to have a painful tooth filled. While her mother was watching a rerun of *Blackmail Me and I'm Yours*, the phone rang.

"Hello?" said Fran's mother, with both eyes fixed on the television screen, where Stacy's brother, Bella, the transvestite, was about to take Marcus' gun from Jerry's drawer, so that he could shoot Joe's best friend, Conrad. The soap opera was getting complicated and she didn't want to miss anything.

"Is this Mrs. Roy?" It was a curt-sounding gentleman with a voice she didn't recognize.

"Yes, it is," answered Fran's mother, forgetting for a moment that it wasn't her house and that Mrs. Roy wasn't her name. "Oh, no, sorry, it's Pam. It's her mom."

"Pam, this is Curt Carrier from the U.S. Postal Service. We are holding weeks of accumulated mail that belongs to your daughter. We have been trying to deliver this mail since the end of March without success." It was a canned voice. The speech was halting, and sounded like a kidnapper reading cut-out words from a ransom note.

"You have what?" asked Pam, just as the television showed Alex walking into the room with Jenny's best friend's brother, David and his wife's second cousin, Theresa (the escort), who was holding a large, gleaming knife with serious intent.

"Pam, we know that you are aware of this mail. Each time we try to deliver it, it either stays in the box for days on end, or it is removed for a day, and then returned back into the mailbox the next day. Sometimes, only certain pieces are removed. We have also found that occasionally some envelopes are opened up, and then taped back together again and placed back into the mailbox. Pam, your daughter can't open her mail and then return the items that she doesn't like."

The sound of a gunshot rang through the room, and Pam momentarily dropped the phone. The TV screen showed John's sister's friend, Betsy, standing in Jerry's office, as she held the smoking gun that she had stolen from Puri's car while she was in the hotel room last Tuesday with Conrad. Robert's half step-sister, Evelyn, suddenly appeared at the door. Conrad was lying by the desk in a pool of blood. Silence. Then a piercing scream.

"Pam? Are you all right?" It was Curt Carrier and his voice was trembling. "Was that a gunshot I just heard?"

"Yes," answered Pam. "Don't worry," she continued, relieved now that Conrad's wheeling and dealing would come to a halt and that Theresa wouldn't have to go to jail. "Everything's taken care of now."

"Pam—you didn't shoot your daughter did you? We, we can work this out without violence. Oh my!" His voice tapered off. A commercial came on and Pam was back into the real world again.

"Shoot my daughter?" exclaimed Pam. "Now there's a thought," she muttered almost inaudibly. "Not yet," she continued, "but I'll make sure this problem is taken care of, don't you worry." The phone went dead in Curt's hand.

The next day he quit his job.

When young Mrs. Roy returned later that afternoon, with one side of her face still holding the grotesque, frozen smile of Novocain, she had several shopping bags hanging from her wrists. "Look what I got on sale!" said Francine, not bothering with the customary, "hello."   Her   mother also kicked all pleasantries aside as she intercepted her daughter's goods like a linebacker stepping in and catching a forward pass. "And I'll take THOSE!" was her warm greeting. "These are going right back!"

"Why?" asked Francine, ready to tackle the interceptor. "What do you mean?"

"Maybe you should be using the money you are spending on clothes to pay your bills!" she challenged.

"I do use the money I spend on clothes to pay the bills. I have money, I buy clothes and then the credit card bills come. The stores have their chance to get their money."

"But is it a fair chance" asked her mother, "when you don't pay them? Isn't it stealing, if you have no intention to pay the stores what you owe?"

Her mother's logic always trapped her in a corner. Francine had nothing more to say, but her mother had a mini-series full.

After dinner, when the macaroni had been picked out of junior's hair, and Marcie had been put down to sleep, they had The Big Talk. The Big Talk was a long time in coming. Poor Fran hadn't committed a terrible crime. It's not like she had killed a man for cheating at cards down Albuquerque way, or anything. If you compare something bad to something terrible, it's a great way to show how small your own crime really is, and it helps ease the guilt tremendously. Fran didn't pick up her mail because she couldn't pay her bills, and until she could pay them, she was going to turn her back on them. It's so much easier to turn your back on something that sits outside, hidden in a mailbox, than something that's already in your home, staring at you with its red-eyed words. When Fran's mother heard her excuse, she was furious.

"But Francine!" reprimanded her mother. "The U.S. Mail never stops coming and you always have to deal with it. That's part of being an American. Just because Bryan isn't contributing to your bills anymore, doesn't mean that you stop paying them."

Just like the guy who killed the man for cheating at cards down Albuquerque way, Fran hung her head in shame.

Two days later, Pam arrived at Fran's house one hour before the bag of mail was due to arrive. The re-delivery fee had been paid, and when they were 45 minutes into their third coffee there was a relentless knocking at the door. Fran's heart began thumping and she couldn't catch her breath. She almost expected to hear, "Open up! It's the FBI. We've emptied your mailbox and blocked all exits to your home. We're going to stand here until you open up all of your mail." But there was no shouting or weapons drawn as Pam opened the door. It was the mailman, and while a marching band struck up on the television for a deodorant commercial, the Great Mail Depositing Ceremony began. It wasn't too bad; only three small bagfuls of mail and a large package containing jewelry from Tiara TV. Oops, bad timing for Francine. She hid the box of jewelry in the palm plant by the front door, while her mother was trying to tip the mailman. "For goodness' sakes, mom." said Fran. "Stop tipping everyone who comes to the door. No wonder you never have any money!"

As the door closed behind the mailman, across the street at number 108 the drapes twitched and even at such an early hour, Mrs. Klatsch picked up her phone to call Mrs. Chismes at number 33. The scandal continued.

As Fran opened her mail she said to Pam, "I don't have the money to pay all of these bills, so what should I do now that I've looked at them?" Real tears of worry ran copiously down the side of her nose and she watched them drop onto the telephone bill, making it soft and wet. She hoped it would rip the paper so that she wouldn't have to pay the bill. She then turned her head towards the gas bill and cried even harder.

Pam told her she would need to change her spending habits. She told Fran to call the utilities, doctors and the credit card companies to let them know that she wasn't avoiding them and that she had some temporary financial problems. When she called them, they helped her set up payment plans until she could get back on her feet, so that each month all of the debtors would receive a portion of what she owed them. Then Pam made her swear that she would never ignore her mail again. Before she left, Fran saw Pam retrieve the box of jewelry hidden in the palm plant by the door and Pam took it home with her. The following week, when Pam visited her daughter, she brought her a special gift to celebrate. Was it a piece of jewelry from the box that was hidden in the palm plant? Nope. That entire box was returned. The gift she gave her daughter was a much smaller mailbox.

Comment

Ignoring things doesn't make them go away, it makes them grow bigger. For example, if you ignore a lowfat healthy diet, you will get bigger. It's the same for many other things, and when you become overwhelmed, it's because you have been ignoring your responsibilities. You have to keep up with things on a daily basis or the results can manifest themselves in a messy house, loss of friends or financial problems. Debts are like a dictator; you need to give them all of your attention early on and nip them in the bud before they take over your world. Stand up to your responsibilities and don't be a slave to anyone. Not even to the US Postal Service.

Happy for a Moment
Removing the gum of unhappiness
from under your shoe

$\mathcal{S}$ top worrying about long-term happiness and have a moment, or several moments that make you really happy. Five seconds, maybe. Can you stretch it to 10 or even 20? Be patient with yourself, don't forget that you may be living from hour to hour right after your breakup. If you can't think of anything that could make you happy, make yourself unhappy, then stop doing it. Wear shoes that are too small for you for an hour or so, then take them off. Aaah, there's the happiness that has been eluding you. Or stretch your arms up over your head until you can't keep them there any longer. Then continue for another 60 seconds. What a great moment when you finally bring them back down.

It's common knowledge that happiness is all around us because we see it in others. Sometimes it's contagious and other times we push it away without realizing it. Why do we repel it? The answer is found in basic chemistry. Many people don't understand chemistry and for them the world is a mysterious place. How can flies magically develop in a garbage can that has a tight lid? But they do. How can a virus or a baby begin as a dot in a Petri dish in a lab? But it's true they can begin their growth there. How can we take a little grain of happiness and make it grow into a good feeling that lasts longer than a few moments? Well, that's the tough part.

The Tale of Mona

Since Mona and her girlfriend Krysten parted ways, Mona felt there was no more happiness in her life. Nothing gave her even a modicum of delight, no dusting of enjoyment, not even a passing whiff of glee. Her life was so empty of joy that she threw herself into her job, and in the evenings she sat with a sad face in front of the television. Nothing made her smile, nothing made her glad, and sadness surrounded her like an umbrella in the rain, with drops of glum falling around her face like confetti.

After working wicked hard all day on Thursday, Mona was on her way home from her grueling job in the Big City, where she ran errands for an architectural firm called Hung, Drawn and Blueprinted. From morning until the end of the business day she delivered blueprints to client's offices, sometimes climbing unforgiving spiral staircases in old buildings and waiting endlessly for subways and buses. In the winter she dodged the rain and freezing snow and in the heat of summer she sweated in an unladylike manner.

This particular Thursday was a broiler. She had been exceptionally busy running here and there in the stifling August sun and its companion, the tireless humidity. The 6 p.m. hour evaded her until the end of the day, and with great relief, she stood waiting on the platform for the 6:10 p.m. train that was coming in from West 4th Avenue. Once the train dragged itself into the station with a hiss of fatigue, Mona picked up her heavy bag, ready to make the commute home. As she attempted to board, a sniffling businessman with ring-around the armpit pushed in front of her. He was carrying an expensive, neglected-looking calf leather briefcase that was pregnant with bulky documents. Using his case as an overweight broomstick, he swept Mona out of the way, pounding her on both kneecaps like a gangster warning a gambler about an unpaid debt.

The pain was all-encompassing as she stumbled onto the train and limped toward the only open seat in the car. Unfortunately, the bully had also seen the seat, and with the last straw sticking in Mona's craw like a badly-chewed crouton, she watched him make his way to the open seat. But then she saw what he did not, which was a melting wad of gum, pink and obscene, shining mischievously and wet on his target seat. His selfish bulk squished the viscous matter as he sat down heavily without looking, and pants met goo.

Mona stood in the train's corridor as the locomotive brought the commuters home, her body being tossed and shaken against the car wall. As she looked out the window and watched the city turn into a forest, she idly felt in her pocket for the rude man's cellphone that had fallen out of his pocket just as he was about to board the train. Mona had picked it up from the station platform, and now she twisted it in her hand like a gunslinger twirling his gun at sundown. She watched smugly as he checked his pockets, his briefcase and his pockets again for his missing phone. Once the temptation of tossing it out of the open window had passed, she was sure that she would hand it back to him soon. Yes, life does have its wonderful moments.

Comment

Take a touch of happiness wherever you may find it, although it's not recommended to take it at someone else's expense.

Happiness is all around us, floating in bits and pieces in the atmosphere. Reach out and grab it wherever you can get it and nurture it, feed it the fertilizer of more happiness and it will grow big and fat. Do things you enjoy. Indulge yourself and concentrate on your own enjoyment, if even for a short while. Stop expecting others to provide happiness for you: your ex-partner, your sympathetic friend, your loyal family.

Grab a crumb of satisfaction wherever you can find it. Smile at an attractive stranger; be cheerful when you find lost money in your jacket pocket; eat more than three chocolates; over-indulge on TV sitcoms. You know best what simple things can make you happy. If all else fails, grab yourself a Petri dish and a measure of artificial cheer. Add a smile from yesterday, or even a smirk will do, then add a cheap laugh and voila! You are halfway to a decent measure of synthesized happiness. Only *you* will know it's not the real thing, but it should be enough to get you started.

Writing It all Down
Graffiti on a notepad

Trying to suppress chaos can be like keeping snakes in a basket. If you take off the lid and look down at them, they will come out. Probably bite you, too, given half a chance. Chaos in a basket is not as dangerous as snakes, but it is more dangerous than chicken in a basket, unless it's the kind that's not quite cooked all the way through. After a breakup, chaos can too-easily follow, and just like poison in your drinking water, everything in your life will soon become affected.

To stop this from happening, you should organize yourself by writing things down. Making lists of problems or things to be done can calm you in the same way as listening to a symphony, but without loud instruments like horns and drums making your heart pound. Reading through a list is not only relaxing to the soul, but also gives you a sense of achievement, even before you start to tackle any of the items that you have written down. You can even cheat by listing tasks you have already completed, just to get you started on the right track, so that you have something to put your first check mark next to.

Other things to write down are worries and bad feelings, because once they have been written down, they become diluted in your head, much like Scotch in a glass of ice, which also makes everything easier to deal with, except for work and reality. Once your problems have been written down, you can either read them back, or tear them up. Putting them away in a box for a while is not a good idea because when you come across them again, believe me, reading them back at a later date will make you sad, and sadness is something that needs to be written down and then torn up and used for kindling. It's a little-known fact that words of sadness make the biggest flames in any fire.

The Tale of Michelle

Jay was always the stability to Michelle's chaos, and when they broke up, it was as though she had put all of her life's confusion neatly into a large trash can to be dealt with later, piece by piece, but then Jay knocked it over when he left. Michelle's life suddenly became confusing and overwhelming with bills spread all over the couch and her clean underwear hanging on the fake Yule log to dry.

Michelle had never been able to carry any chore through from beginning to end because something would always come along to distract her. Last week she was folding clothes in the bedroom when she heard something rustling in the kitchen. On her way to investigate, she slid on a magazine that was on the floor, and as she fell onto her left elbow, her right arm flew up into the air. As her fall continued down onto the rug, out of the corner of her eye she saw her checkbook on the nightstand, and, remembering that it was time to pay the power bill, she grabbed it as she fell. Sitting on the floor, rubbing her elbow and holding her checkbook, she noticed some spilled popcorn under the bed and reached out to pick it up. A rank smell wafted toward her and she realized she needed to take a shower.

She passed the cactus on her way to the shower and noticed that it needed water, and she headed to the kitchen. The mystery of what was rustling in there an hour ago was solved as she watched her notes from her creative writing class continue to blow out of the open window into John and Jerry's oak tree next door. The power bill never was paid that month. The popcorn stayed under the bed until she dropped her contact lens and rediscovered the kernels under the bed; but luckily the cactus lived, even though it had to wait until July to be watered.

Michelle was in need of a list; or many lists. She was becoming overwhelmed and exhausted.

While still married, she and Jay visited a marriage counselor a few months before their relationship gave a sad little hiss and collapsed. The counselor was a strong advocate of recording everything on paper. Until then, Michelle hadn't written much down at all since she left school, except for shopping lists and that one time she wrote some graffiti on the wall outside a bar when she was drunk. Optimistic with the advice the counselor had given them several months ago, she dug out a pen from Dual City Bank, found a notepad and started thinking.

Her first lists were on plain paper, but because she found that a little depressing, she started to decorate the lists with stickers of angels and cute puppies because that was what she liked to look at to cheer herself up. To keep it interesting, she developed a points system where she awarded herself points each day if she made progress on getting her life back together. Once she reached 20 points, she surprised herself with a gift. The first list Michelle put together covered one week. It began on a Saturday and looked like this, except with numerous spelling mistakes:

Moods: Watching a commercial for hair loss made me cry because it made me think about Jay.

The House: Cleaning the kitchen, I finally threw out the avocados from the refrigerator and wiped up the slime.

Making An Effort: I'm trying to eat less fast food. I went out and bought more avocados. Must remember to look up the guacamole recipe before they go bad again.

Being Proud of Myself: I didn't check my cell phone every five minutes to see if Jay called. I stretched it to every 10 minutes.

Socializing: I called Sheila to remind her that she owes me $15.

Recovery: I felt better this afternoon than I did in the morning (not as sad).

Things to Do (She wanted to write, "Activities," but she couldn't spell it.): I went for a walk for the first time in a week.

Why I am Better Off Without Jay: I can watch the fashion shows on television any time I like without listening to Jay making fun of the Iris Brothers' commentary.

Don't make the mistake of listing the bad things that could make you sad. They are alive and well in your head and you need to exterminate them, so put them on the cleaning out list, along with the roach killer.

Michelle's lists might show minor things, but her good points added up and pretty soon she had awarded herself a nice, inexpensive gift from an online jewelry store. Maybe a week ago she didn't feel like bringing the garbage out, and at that time, she wasn't in the mood to call Sheila, so minor steps in the right direction became big steps to her and earned her two points, not to mention $15. Obviously, different people struggle more with different things.

Comment

You too can be like Michelle. When you can't solve a problem, or too many things are adding up in your mind and keeping you awake at night, write them down. Once they are written down, read them out loud and then try to solve them without any emotion, and then give yourself some guidance. The difficult part would be taking the advice. I mean, look at the source, it's not like you are an expert or anything. But make sure that you act upon it, you know how you are.

But when all's said and done, making a list is just as absolving as going to the priest and a whole lot less embarrassing.

Friends, From Ours to Yours
Unlike candy, friends are not for sharing

*I*n what situation (besides a gay one) does the boy get the boy, and the girl gets the girl? Answer: when a husband and wife are friends with another man and woman and one of the couples breaks up. Often, the males of the couples initially remain buddies with each other and the females stay friends. But a change in partner status can affect this balance and someone always gets left out. The law tries to be fair and clear on dividing up property when you divorce, but it doesn't reference the divvying up of mutual friends. It's legal to pilfer your ex-partner's friends, but is it ethical?

The Tale of Anna

Anna and Jonas were a sociable couple. They had many friends together, but no friends individually. That's pretty common when you are in a relationship, but a very bad thing after you break up. It's always good to have Friends Insurance, which is another way of saying that you maintained your own friends during your relationship and didn't share them with your partner.

When you were together you didn't care about spending time with your boring friends, since you had your man, Constantine the handsome Greek to spend every hour of the day and night with. Such was the situation with Anna, except her handsome man was named Jonas and he was Irish-American.

Friends were the last thing on Anna's mind as she tried to put her life back together after the breakup with Jonas. She spent her days missing him and the evenings were swollen with the loss of him. Consequently, all her time was taken up thinking about Jonas.

It was 5 p.m. on Sunday evening when Anna walked into her kitchen with a small cache of dirty snack plates in her hand. She was usually a clean person, but since their breakup, her housekeeping enthusiasm was on hiatus, sitting with its feet propped up on the couch, watching comedy shows on cable.

The little grey mouse didn't look up from its meal of yesterday's rice pudding as Anna put the plates down in the sink. But when she uttered a gasp, it turned its head slowly and gave her the evil mouse eye. Then it continued eating. Its long pink tail rested on the house phone and little brown parcels of poo that she had never noticed before decorated the stovetop in a hap-hazard manner. Some were a little melted from the heat of the cooking.

Backing out of the kitchen, she reached for her cell phone on the coffee table. Wiping off the crumbs from the dial pad, she called Jonas. Who else was there to call? He was a man and so much bigger than a mouse. He didn't answer. Who else could she call? She dialed Lindsay and Curtis' number and Lindsay answered.

"Hi Lindsay," she said. "Can you and Curtis come over right away? There's a mouse in my kitchen and I'm terrified."

There was a long pause at the other end of the phone, and then some muffled whispering. She heard Lindsay say "I can't. You do it."

Then a muffled voice said, "Pass me the phone over."

"Hi Anna," said Curtis." What's up?"

"Hi Curtis. Well, there's a mouse in my kitchen. Will you please come over and put it outside for me? I have a terrible fear of mice."

Anna was surprised when she heard Curtis' reply. "Sorry Anna, I can't do that. You see, Lindsay and I are friends with Jonas."

"Yes," said Anna. "You are friends with Jonas and me. Have been for eight years."

"Well, that's the problem," he continued. "We felt we had to pick sides and Jonas needs a friend right now. We don't want to upset him more than he already is."

Anna was shocked. "But Jonas broke up with me when he met Gracie. *I'm* the one who's upset!"

There was a thoughtful pause. It was going to be a compromise.

"I have an idea," he said. "I'll ask Jonas if he minds if we come over just this once, and if he says yes, we'll be right there."

"But what if he says no?" asked Anna.

"Then I'm afraid we will have to break all ties with you."

Anna was incredulous. "But then I'll have been double-dumped!"

"I'm sorry, Anna. I'll talk to Jonas and maybe just this once we can help you out." The line went dead and so did Anna's mood.

"I'll show them," she thought to herself. "I'll call Joanna and Derek."

Anna tried to stay calm, but she was mad as a bad temper as she dialed Joanna's number. The mouse just gloated and began lapping a soft puddle of bacon fat that was spilt at breakfast.

"Joanna, hi. It's Anna. I wondered if you and Derek could do me a favor. You see there's a mouse in my kitchen and I can't reach an exterminator until tomorrow morning. Could you and Derek come over and take care of it for me? Please? It's just a little one," she wheedled.

"Anna, hi," came Joanna's voice. "A mouse, huh? That's some back luck. No, we're sorry we can't help you. It wouldn't be fair to Jonas and Gracie."

Anna choked. "Jonas and Gracie! What do you mean? You are my friend from high school. We have known each other for years before you even met Jonas."

Joanna sighed. "I know," she commiserated, "but Jonas is depressed at the moment and he needs his friends. He called us the day you guys broke up because he wanted us to be there for him."

Anna thought this a little sneaky of Jonas. "How about me?" she complained. I need a friend, too. Not just to help with the mouse, but a real friend. Forever."

"I'm so sorry Anna. I know how you feel, but you'll make plenty of new friends really soon. You're very outgoing. Oh, and good luck with your mouse. Take care, bye."

Was this really happening to her? Did Jonas really steal their two best couple friends? But that was the problem, they were couple friends and Anna was no longer a couple. Jonas was. He had wasted no time in gathering up their friends and turning them against her. And that Gracie—she was a sneaky, good-for-nothing…

Suddenly the mouse ran over her hand then stopped at the breakfast cereal bowl and started lapping up the milk.

She stared at its little pink feet. Was this little mouse to be her only friend now? Of course not. If she didn't clean up the kitchen soon, she would have many more little four legged rodent friends.

Comment

Jonas had been sneaky and stolen their couple friends, even those she had before they met. After their breakup, she was not only cast out by Jonas, like they did in the bible back in The Day, but also cast out by all of the friends that Jonas knew.

The story continues on a sadder note. Not only did Anna lose Jonas, Lindsey and Curtis, and the rest of their mutual friends, she had forgotten to take out Friends Insurance when she met Jonas. Friends Insurance is offered by your old friends from school, Ed and Cindy, your neighbor Betty, and Adam from the gym. Or any other friends you spent time with before your big relationship came sailing into the bay like a cruise ship ready to take you away on the trip of a lifetime. Now that the ship has docked and everyone has disembarked, where are your friends? Are they waiting at the port, ready to welcome you back? What? You didn't even send them a postcard from the Ports of Happiness, New Boyfriend or Engagement? What makes you think they will be there to greet you now?

Anna had to reclaim her old friends—and fast. She was afraid to call them after so long, but she tried. She emailed them and told them she had a new email address, which she really only got as an excuse to contact them. She sent out "Just A Note To Say Hi" cards with her new address and phone number, inviting them to call her and telling them she would be back in touch. Humble pie tastes much better than Nofriends pie, which tastes like sawdust with cobwebs in it, but it had to be done. Luckily, many of these people were hoping their lives had turned out better than hers, and they were thrilled to find out that theirs had. But she didn't tell them that pretty soon she would have a new kick-ass fabulous life again, plus a host of new friends that she would keep in touch with, come hell or high water, and a fabulous new boyfriend.

So then, what else happened to Anna? She eventually ended up happy. While at the gym one evening she bumped into Tomas, another old friend. They hit it off immediately and began dating. Ironically, Tomas was Jonas' best friend. Correction, he *used to be* Jonas' best friend. After all, Jonas owed her at least a few of his own friends.

10 Pointers to Prepare Yourself for Dating Again

1: Confidence

eing in a relationship may have made you half an item because your partner was the other half. Some relationships are not equal, and you may have found yourself being the insignificant half instead of the better half. This inequality and lack of presence might have drained your confidence, after all, part of you is missing somewhere in the cracks of the breakup, along with some of your self-assurance.

Comment

It's like a lizard losing its tail. When you lose part of yourself, you have to grow back to being a whole person again. It's another of the miracles of nature, like kangaroos with pockets and crabs walking sideways. So, like the lizard without a tail, or the snake that sheds its skin, you will become whole again. That's great news, especially considering you are not a reptile. So until you get all of those functioning parts back, pretend you have all of the confidence you started with, and lie with conviction.

2: Psyching yourself up

You are persuading yourself to go out and meet some new people. Your enthusiasm is bursting out all over and consequently you are dousing yourself with fragrance. You are having too many drinks before leaving the house. You wash your hair with cynicism and wear a new coat of indifference. You are ready to meet your friends and party!

Comment

Don't think that psyching yourself up means exaggerating everything. That's only the case in sports. Moderate amounts of all things are best, with only a sprinkling of cynicism and indifference. And go easy on the perfume or cologne.

3: Asking for Advice

Being newly single is like being unable to hear. There is silence all around you. Maybe it's because your jabbering, television-watching mate has departed. Getting used to being single again is like slowly getting your hearing back. After the silence, there is sound, but everything is muffled and you can't understand what's being said. What can you do? You ask your friends "How do I behave now that I'm single again? What should I do if…? Why is…?" and other mystifying questions. They try to tell you how to get your life back under control. They tell you how to behave. They tell you to keep away from your ex. They tell you, "Have I got the one for you!"

Comment

Take your friends with a grain of salt. Once a day, after dinner with a large glass of wine.

4: Who is out there?

Your friends have dragged you out and who is out there? Members of the opposite sex. Why do we call them members? Can we join their club? So who are these people? And are they really The Opposite?

Comment

Yep. Couldn't be more opposite. Members of the opposite sex might seem very alien to you now. You are used to dealing with Partner, Family, Friends of the Same Sex and Familiar Co-Workers. Period. Be kind to these alien beings of the opposite sex. Try talking to them, ask them questions about themselves, and then you will find out who they are and they will morph into humans. You may find the male/female differences enticing once again and if you don't yet, you will. Your friends can't be that wrong. They may be all you have. And as for the members part, you cannot join their club. It's exclusive and you must have the right anatomy.

5: Where to meet people

You are all dressed up to go out, but where do you go to meet that next special someone? You have heard of all of the places that are popular, and you used to go to similar ones when you were single, but where do you go now?

Comment

People are hooking up all over the place. How hard can it be? You have to educate yourself. Ask around or go out with friends; read the local newspaper for local events; look online for safe singles; join a group you have something in common with, even if you only go out with them one time. Take on another job a couple of nights a week or volunteer, you'll meet people. Girls, go to the hardware store; guys, go to the grocery store and kill two birds with one stone.

6: Smiling

You've heard about this, but are reluctant to try it. Older people tell you it's the best way to catch someone's eye, but you are unsure.

Comment

Smiling IS the best way to meet someone. It's contagious, like watching someone yawn or have sex (as the porn movie makers have proved). Pretty soon you'll want to do it too. The same applies to smiling. If you smile at someone, chances are upon pure instinct they'll smile back. These are subtle starts to getting someone's attention, and if they reciprocate, you could be on a roll.

7: Conversation with a Stranger

You see someone you like, but what do you say?

Comment

Like smiling, saying "hi" is contagious, too. Then you could make small talk, which consists of stating the obvious, and if done right, won't make you seem as stupid as it sounds. Talk about the weather or something related to where you are standing. If you meet with a cold response or none at all, move on. If your comment of "it's cold today" is responded to with repetition "yes, it's cold today" that person is either unimaginative or married, and is only being polite. You may want to skip that one. You could be lucky and meet someone who is chatty about the weather or if they don't have much to say, they may smile and make eye contact, which is your cue to continue.

8: Not knowing how to behave socially
as a single anymore

Flirting doesn't come naturally to you, nor does talking to strangers. Does it show if you feel depressed? How do you not look awkward? When do you make eye contact? When do you offer to accept or buy a drink? How close do you stand to someone if you like them? Can you paw a stranger you would like to spend the night with before you have spoken with them?

Comment

You shouldn't have forgotten all of your social etiquette, unless you have been living on a mountaintop and have now only just returned to the Big City. Look around you and see how others are behaving. Don't stand too close to people and don't be pushy. If someone is having a conversation with their friends, smile, or say "hi," but don't interrupt them. Touching someone should be taken slowly and generally never used on a complete stranger. And guys, if you are in a bad part of town, some people may allow you to touch them for money. It might be wise to not take them up on this offer, because it's illegal. Ask a prospective date what they are comfortable with if you don't know or can't figure it out.

9: Self Esteem–gone today, here tomorrow

You've finally met another someone, but how do you know if you have low self-esteem? Will they think you have a low opinion of yourself, and if so, should it matter to them when they like you anyway?

Comment

If you speak badly to someone about yourself they will probably believe you, after all, who knows you better than you do? If you speak highly of yourself to someone, even if you don't really believe it, they will probably accept it as being true—at least until they know you better and by then, you will have convinced them of how great you really are. No one wants to be around someone who doesn't like themselves. What's the point of that? Another indication of low self-esteem is if you feel sorry for the person you are dating. Then it's time to try self-suggestion, where you tell yourself over and over again how wonderful you are and how lucky your date is. Buy yourself a gift to prove your magnificence. Chocolates are nice.

10: Going out and staying out—the anti-frisbee rule

You don't ever want to go out and mingle again. You want to stay home and think about your ex all night and every night. Your friends talk you into going out. It's a big effort for you: showering, looking nice, being polite, switching off the TV set. You go, but then half an hour later, you want to go back home. This is part of being newly-single. It's like trying to fight a slow strangulation.

Comment

Once you start getting itchy feet that want to wander home, you really should stay out and at least give the evening a little more effort. Tell your friends you will be leaving in 30 minutes, and that will force you to hang on just a bit longer, which will make going out easier next time. Also, the longer you stay out with your friends, the less time they will have to talk about you behind your back.

PART FIVE

HEALING

A Keg of Independence, Dating and Rebuilding

Feeling Sorry for Yourself
Sampling the breakup diet

D o you remember those old gangster movies where the mobster gives the poor patsy a pair of concrete shoes and throws him into the river? They hit bottom quickly, and it's pretty low. Once you have sunk that far, there's nowhere deeper down to go. Out on dry land there's also a bottom to the earth and many who have been there call it rock bottom, on account of there being many rocks there. You don't just sink to rock bottom, you hit rock bottom and it hurts like hell, which is even further down.

So there you are, all the way down to rock bottom. You try to claw your way up and it feels like you are being buried alive, but without the dirt. You want to escape, but you don't have the strength; the light in your life has diminished and there's sadness at the corner of your eyes that feels like sand, but it's probably just an irritating grain of heartache. You are feeling sorry for yourself, and when people say you are wallowing in self-pity, it means you are enjoying it just a little bit. Why else would you keep on doing it? Because it's easier to do it than not to do it. Let's face it, you are sad.

The Tale of Tracy

When people diet, they substitute celery for ice cream. When they stop smoking, they substitute chewing gum for a cigarette. When they stop drinking alcohol, they substitute an AA meeting for a shot of bourbon. When someone breaks up with you, you substitute ice cream, cigarettes and bourbon for their love. That works for a while, and then you have to substitute all of those things for a healthier lifestyle. So you are not only coping with a lost love, you are coping with an addiction to food and chemicals. Lucky you!

Tracy was at the beginning of an addiction to ice cream, cigarettes and bourbon when Shawn left her and moved back to Canada. She also had a Shawn-sized hole in her heart on the day he left, wearing his cowboy hat and looking like a hero from a blockbuster movie. Standing at the door waving him goodbye, or au revoir, as they say in Quebec, she felt hungry. Her hunger was for sadness, so she fed the sadness-hunger by missing him every second of the day. After a while, hunger for food came along and she made herself a meal. After that, a strange hunger gripped her entire body that came from a lack of love and she didn't know how to feed it.

She played solitaire, drank too much alcohol and stayed up almost all night. On Saturday she felt hung-over and ate greasy food and felt somewhat better. So there was a solution, feed the hunger, even if you're not hungry for food. Substitute food for love. She began to eat more and while she ate she was happy for a while. Eating is wonderful, she said to herself. It's as good as watching television. In fact, what a great combination! So then she began to sit around the apartment, watching TV and over-eating, and it was amazing how much she was able to consume after a while. Her stomach grew and grew, and the two pieces of pie she ate after dinner, turned into three and four as time went by, and her appetite became ever-increasing, as did her diameter and circumference.

One day, she thought about going to the flea market or out for a walk and that made her feel better. Unfortunately, by the time she had eaten two big slices of pizza, she forgot all about getting out of the apartment. After three pieces of chocolate cake, she was determined to do those things the next day, and while she wondered what to have for dessert, she uncurled herself from the couch and fetched a pen, a pad of paper, and an economy-sized bag of sea salt potato chips.

Engrossed in her snacks, her mind wandered and she realized that coming home to an empty home was extremely depressing; not only because she was now living alone, but also because it made her sad that the apartment looked exactly the same when she arrived home, as it did when she left it each morning. Of course that's typical when you live alone, unless a burglar visited while you were at work and ransacked the place, then it would look different. Initially, there might be more of a mess to clean up and several more drawers to close, but fewer items of value to put back on top of the mantel or into the jewelry box.

Coming home to a messy, lonely home is no fun, but it's so much worse when your love has recently left you. Instead of being greeted at the door by a partner with a smile and a gift, you are greeted by no one, except perhaps your dog, Toby, and goodness knows you don't want to receive a gift from him. That would require even more cleaning up. So you unlock your door, step into your home and wade through the dirty clothes on the floor toward the kitchen. While still wearing your coat and shoes you wash one necessary bowl and a spoon from the dirty stack in the kitchen sink, scoop out some chocolate chip mint ice cream and then sit down, putting your grimy street feet up on top of the unopened bills that are lying on your coffee table. Welcome Home! It's enough to make you want to turn heel and walk right back out again, which some of us do. But at some point you have to come back home.

This was the predicament Tracy faced every time she went through her apartment door. Looking at the neglected mess made her so much more depressed and her layers of depression expanded like puff pastry and gave her an appetite for apple turnovers, beef wellington, and those little puffy Greek goat cheese and spinach triangles—spanakopita. She had nothing else to look forward to, and keeping herself occupied by doing housework while she was in a state of hopelessness just wasn't to be. The depression zapped her energy and the less she did around the apartment, the worse everything became. She needed something to cheer her up and she lacked encouragement that family and friends could provide because they weren't around. She was on her own.

But Tracy was a creative and smart girl and she hit upon a good idea to eliminate the ongoing misery of slap-across-the-face loneliness when she first opened her front door after work. As cleaning and straightening was not yet in the cards, she decided to give herself a pleasant surprise each time she came home from work. That way she would be in a better frame of mind to meet her empty home each evening and make tackling those intimidating and abandoned household chores a possibility.

This was her plan. She put a small table where it would be the first thing she saw when she opened her front door. Every evening she would stage it with something to look forward to the following evening when she came home from work. Her experiment began on Sunday evening, when she placed various items on the little table: A miniature bottle of coffee liquor, a CD she hadn't yet listened to and a menu from her favorite pizza place. When she came home from work on Monday evening, all crabby and ready to be lonely and depressed, the items on her table were the first thing she saw when she opened her door.

It seemed a bit corny at first, but it made her smile just a little bit. Now she had something of a normal evening to look forward to. It wasn't dinner out with Shawn or a kiss in the kitchen, but it might help diminish the overeating and it was a basic plan for the dreaded Monday night. Later on that evening while she still had a smile on her face, and right before she went to bed, she picked up her clothes from the bedroom floor and put them in the hamper. Then she again staged the small table for the following night.

When she arrived home from work the next day, Tuesday's "surprise" revealed two folded pieces of paper on the table, along with her headphones and music and a box of fudge cake mix. She opened one of the folded notes and it read, "Go to the gym." Because she had written it only 19 hours prior, she remembered that the other piece of paper read, "Take a walk in the park." As no one was around to catch her cheating, she refolded the first note and opened the other one. What a surprise! A walk in the park! That sounded better than going to the gym, especially as it would be followed by dinner and a slice or two of warm chocolate cake. She had also left herself information about a late-night vampire movie on TV that she had seen many times, but wanted to see again.

Later on that evening her energy came back somewhat (maybe it was due to the chocolate cake) and she washed five days worth of dishes, tried her new hand cream for her pruned fingertips, then staged the table for another "surprise." Coming home on Wednesday evening she was greeted by a note that she had written to herself, allowing her to buy $50 worth of real or electronic books, and next to the note was a small bag of baked chips and lowfat dip and a miniature candy bar. Considerately allowing herself a compromise, she spent $25 on books and $25 on makeup, instead of the whole $50 on books. Online shopping within a budget removed her from the temptation of too much television and an evening of overeating.

Thursday evening followed, which was her favorite television night. She left herself a copy of the TV Guide, popcorn and a menu from the new Mexican restaurant on Clemente Avenue, where she would go to pick up her dinner then come back home to watch her shows.

Wanting to challenge herself by the end of the week, she sneakily left out a brochure she had received in the mail with information on a singles night that was being held the following month. Added to that were coupons from a few stores at the mall where she liked to shop. A note from herself, reminding her a slice of chocolate chip cheesecake was in the freezer for when she came back from the mall, completed the package.

That whole week she treated herself to some simple things in life, but placed everything on the table right at the door to greet her the moment she came home. Keeping herself busy and giving herself focus was allowing her to have some much needed direction in her life and strangely enough, it made her feel less lonely and less inclined to binge.

When she ran out of ideas, she made a list of everything she liked and the little and big things that made her happy. It didn't compensate for the loss of Shawn, but somehow it cheered her up every lonely evening. Planning these treats became almost as much fun as receiving them and she didn't even need to write any thank you notes! After a couple of weeks, she was feeling noticeably better and more motivated to do those forgotten household chores she had been putting off for too long. Planning her evenings this way was like having a date with herself, but not having to worry if she would order the priciest dish on the menu, or have to fight off a groper in the hallway. She was trying to move on with her life and found that at times, she wasn't sad at all. A little bit of sunshine now greeted her when she opened up the door to her home.

Comment

Getting over a partner who left you is a journey, rather than a destination, so you have to prepare for that trip and start packing ahead of time. Of course your suitcase is only meta-phorical, so it can be any color. Simply put, when the depression momentarily lifts, prepare yourself for that time when you are down again—that time when sadness pushes you against the wall like a thug in an alleyway. Unhappiness, like any illness can be debilitating, but when you feel good set yourself up for a little comfort for when you don't. Buy yourself a movie, but save it for a bad day. Shop for a steak ahead of time and freeze it, then defrost and cook it when you feel down, and eat it while you watch the movie you put away. Upgrade your cable TV or purchase electronics to keep yourself on a cheerful level. Go shopping at a discount store with only the amount of money in your pocket that you can afford to spend. If it's too much effort to pick up a book and you are tired of television, try an audio book from the library. Learn a language for when you take that weekend trip to Mexico in two year's time, so that you have something to look forward to.

Friends, family and co-workers can be invaluable at this time for support, so never say no to an invitation, no matter how lame the event may seem. Call people you've been neglecting lately, it's great to keep in touch. Walk—in the woods, by your home, anywhere, just to be outside.

The more you physically and mentally do, the less time there is for your thoughts to run free and loose, like Chinese tea. Thinking about how sad you are is self-indulgent and self-destructive. Turn depression into doing. Take out the letters, "D O I N" from the word, "Depression," and add the "G." Now you have "Doing!" So what is left of "Depression?" The letters, "E P R E S S." Now you have yourself an anagram game, and being sad is all but forgotten. Take what you need from your depression, close it up and call it a day. You can live without it.

It's a good idea to take advantage of the time when you feel a little happier and more energetic to prepare yourself for the despondent times, when you just have to watch the rain or look at the old photos to make yourself sad. So get a pet. Watch a good movie on television. Sign up for a class. Put a little table by the door to encourage and reward yourself and soon you may end up being the glue on the fly paper of happiness that attracts everyone to you. Then you can stop hating those happy people with their sympathy smiles and their "have a nice day" attitudes, because it may be their turn to recover from a breakup. You can look them in the eye and sagely say, "I know how you feel. I've been down that road myself. How about sharing some of that chocolate with me?" Don't get too cheerful though, nobody likes a wise guy.

Being Sick Alone
Surviving the jungle of suburban influenza

It feels like the sun will never stop shining its burning heat down on you. Your body is sweating, but feels like ice to the touch. You hear strange animal sounds around you, lions growling, exotic birds whistling and tree monkeys screeching. The jungle is all around you, the heat is oppressive and you can barely place one foot in front of the other to take a step toward saving yourself. Your heart is pounding, you have a thirst that only the desert can bring on and no water is within your reach. Is this a survival story of a man stranded on a desert island? No, it's you when you get the flu. The animal noises you hear are the wheezing in your chest; the whistling is coming from your stuffy nose; and the screeching monkey is a hoarse sneeze that hits the back of your throat. You are sick and living alone and you might as well be stranded on a desert island, because there's no one around to bring you that glass of water you so desperately need.

The Tale of Jayden

Jayden was suffering from the flu. He had staggered into the doctor's office where a fever of 101 was confirmed, bronchitis was beginning and a sore throat added itself to the list of maladies without being asked. He had broken up with Chloe in the summer, and now, in the winter, he was suffering his illness all alone. He was too sick to worry about who was going to take care of him, but the night before, when the nagging fear of illness disturbed his well-being, he remembered something that a wise man had once told him in the dead of winter when fevers ran high and so did doctor's bills. He ran out to the grocery store. He bought juice, aspirins, TV dinners, crackers, soup, paper tissues, cereal bars and fruit. Like a squirrel in the wintertime he stocked his pantry full of food and waited to see if he felt better. It wasn't to be and the visit to the doctor's office the following day confirmed his fears.

He put himself to bed with the phone next to him and felt isolated because no one knew that he was sick and there was no one to help him get through the next few days. He was alone in the jungle of suburban influenza. As he lay in bed with water and crackers next to him, he dozed in and out of consciousness. His mind drifted back to the last time an illness was in his life, but that time it was Chloe, and not he, who was the patient.

It was last November when Chloe had the sniffles and she insisted it was pneumonia. Jayden wasn't convinced, but he drove her to the doctor anyway. Doctor Jackson told her it was a light cold and to drink plenty of fluids, and no, she didn't need any medication because she wasn't sick enough. Feeling that she was at death's door, she took the rest of the day off work and staggered up the stairs to bed, insisting Jayden take her arm in case she fell in her weakened state. He put her to bed, brought her juice, lozenges, extra blankets and fluffed up her pillows.

"I'm hungry," she whispered weakly.

"What can I get you?" he asked her, sympathetically.

"Well, something light," she responded. "Maybe two scrambled eggs. Oh, and two pieces of toast—wait—make that three pieces. And a waffle, but just one, with butter and syrup. Some orange juice and some coffee. A glass of water and two aspirins. The TV Guide. I think that might do it." After everything was done, it was too late for Jayden to go into work, but anyway, Chloe insisted he stay home with her just in case she had to be driven to the hospital.

At the end of the evening, Jayden felt more exhausted than his hypochondriacally inclined patient. She dozed on and off and at 2 a.m. suddenly seemed quite perky. "Jayden," she whispered as he slept. No response. "Jayden!" she said loudly, kicking him under the covers like a mule with a leg cramp.

"What is it?" he asked her. He was groggy, half asleep.

"I'm thirsty. Will you get me a glass of water?" Jayden struggled up out of bed. "I'm a little hungry too. Would you make me a peanut butter and jelly sandwich on wheat toast and a hot tea? I feel so shivery and feverish."

Jayden reluctantly left the safe haven of his cozy bed, trading soft, warm sheets for a chilly kitchen with a cold floor. He returned to his love who was reclining in the bed, wide awake and watching TV. Mothy, her tabby cat had set up his bed on Jayden's pillows and as Jayden came back into the room, Mothy turned his head to look at him disdainfully, and gave a little spit in his direction before turning his head back again toward the television.

"There's your snack," said Jayden, as he put the tray on the bed. "Can I get you anything else?" Chloe sat up and surveyed the room like the queen of the ants, ready to set the underlings to work.

"I'm feeling so ill and exhausted," she said, her face looking a picture of health. "Perhaps some cold and flu medication."

"Maybe we should take your temperature?" suggested Jayden, with a smidgen of irony adding a little-needed chill to the room. "You might have a fever."

"I'm sure I do," responded Chloe, "but I'm way too exhausted to do that right now. I'll just have my sandwich and tea and then if you don't mind, I really need to get some rest. Maybe you should sleep on the couch, that way you won't disturb us."

Mothy turned around with what looked like a triumphant feline grin on his furry face as Jayden walked out of the room and prepared for a chilly night alone on the couch.

Three hours later the alarm clock rang and Chloe was standing over him while he lay on his makeshift bed. "Time to get up," she reminded him.

He sat up. "Are you going into work today?" he asked her.

She felt her forehead Cleopatra-like with the back of her hand. "I'm feverish and I'm not strong enough," she mumbled, overacting just a little. "In fact, I think I'm too weak to stand up much longer. But if you are making yourself a breakfast, I'll have a couple of eggs over easy and just one of those frozen waffles with fresh strawberries, because I need fruit when I'm sick, and of course a glass of orange juice. But not that boxed stuff, some freshly squeezed. The oranges are in the refrigerator."

Jayden was more than a little late to work that day and a whole lot more tired. Chloe called him half a dozen times to ask him she should she go to the doctor? Can she take a vitamin C supplement with an aspirin? Would she feel better if the heat was lowered or if it was turned up? And so on, until Jayden found himself becoming sick of her.

When he arrived home from work, the place looked as though a band of robbers had been given three minutes to find items of value and then vacate the house. Blankets and magazines were strewn on the armchair and aspirins were scattered around like analgesic confetti, with a trail of them leading into the kitchen. Paper handkerchiefs were thrown randomly onto the floor, while in the bathroom, a fine white dust of nail filings made a line of simulated cocaine around the sink, needing just a scale and some baggies for it to resemble a drug dealer's packaging area.

As Jayden began his evening of slave labor, he picked up an aspirin from behind a couch cushion and popped it into his mouth. He took a swig of leftover soup from a pan in the kitchen, along with two vitamin C capsules that were perched atop an open package of bread. He would need all of his strength that evening, along with a homemade potion of patience.

So what did the wise man tell Jayden in the dead of winter? Did he tell him to prepare himself in case a sickness came along and took away all of his strength? No. Did he tell him about a potent batch of secret herbs that would fight the fever and kill the cough? No. He spoke much wiser words. He told him "Man, you need to dump that broad." Thus, spoke Wei Long, the wise man, and he knew about such things, because he had twice met Chloe. As Jayden lay in a fog of the flu, he wondered how she would manage her next illness without him. He really didn't care, but it was the only thing that made him smile while he was feeling totally wretched.

Comment

Why do we demand attention when we are sick? Are we pity-seekers or do we need someone to be our strength when we are weak and defenseless? Illness makes us tired and it might be the only time in our lives when we can be cared for by others. We crave indulgence, and it's not just for the rich, it's for the sick, too!

Some people can resign themselves to being ill and take it in stride. What's the point of feeling sorry for yourself? Your body will reduce your capabilities, but you already know that. You'll be tired and maybe in pain, so be conscious of your limitations and do only what your body allows in your weakened state. It's fine to be ill alone. You don't need an audience for that.

A last minute survival plan would be to organize yourself before you climb into bed. A big bottle of water, a box of tissues, and pack of plain cookies or crackers will get you through a day when you can barely walk and no one is around to take care of you. Keep the phone by the bed and something to read, or the remote control. While you are healthy, shop for canned soup, canned fruit and crackers and put some bread in the freezer in case the day comes when you are too sick to leave the house. With those kinds of supplies you could last a while in the jungle, as long as you don't share your food with the monkeys.

Online Dating
Picking the Right Person: Take a number and get in line

How easy is it to look at a photograph of someone smilingly dressed in their best clothes and guess their personality? Probably almost impossible, but people are doing it all the time online. "But there's a description!" you cry. "It tells you all about them." Not quite. There is no such thing as a fool-proof profile. People can lie about everything, and some people do. The story below tells of someone with bad judgment. Unfortunately, like all people who are bad judges of character, Leanne felt herself to be a good judge of character. Sometimes a good gut feeling about someone is only the result of a heavy meal. Picking a partner is often hit-and-miss and it's even harder to do online.

The Tale of Leanne

Leanne was of average intelligence, often capable enough to get the jobs she applied for and able to watch the news without asking, "I don't understand how you can launder money, won't the print come off?" She was also street-wise and knew not to give strangers a ride when they said their car broke down, and when walking home alone in the dark, she knew to keep looking around her for trouble. She was also housekeeping-savvy and never mixed the dark colored clothes with the light ones, and the pan rarely burned when she cooked. There were also things she excelled at, like sports and art. But the thing she was best at was picking the wrong guy. Her online dating profile stated that she was an animal lover, liked surprises and had a good sense of humor.

Paul had a well-constructed online profile. His photograph showed a man with good looks, brown, curly hair and one of those cute little beards that some ladies liked to tug on. He stated that he was an animal lover. Leanne thought he might be the one to marry.

Their first date went well, and Paul the animal lover invited Leanne back to his place afterward for a coffee and to meet his dogs, Vypah, Broote, and Feend. Paul had described Vypah to her after she had been intimidated by the name. "Oh, it's just a pet name," explained Paul. "He's a very placid dog to have around the house and the name is more of a joke, like a Chihuahua named Killer, that kind of thing. I'm sure you'll like him. All of my dogs are mellow."

When they reached his house, Leanne heard a deep bellowing coming from inside, that sounded like a team of starving wolves fighting over an injured moose. Paul had told Leanne that he was very proud of his dogs, but he didn't tell her that his dogs were proud of themselves. Vypah was so proud of his long, yellow teeth that he showed them off to Leanne all evening long. Broote was proud of his loud, blood-curdling growl, and entertained Leanne with his dog-song until Paul threatened him with a rolled-up newspaper. Feend was covered in scars, and bald patches decorated his body and somehow Leanne knew he was bragging about being the best fighter of them all.

The next day, she took "Animal Lover" off her online profile, and then looked for another date.

Josh was proud of his generosity and his profile stated that he was a giving person. Leanne thought he might be the one to marry. He seemed so kind that his homely looks could be overlooked. When they first met, Josh handed Leanne a long, black velvet box. When she opened it, she saw it was a silver bracelet. She was taken aback. "Thank you so much," she stammered. "This is so kind of you."

"Kindness is my middle name!" joked Josh, and Leanne thought him such a generous man.

It was the same on every date. One box was round and held a ring. One was square and held a gold pin with diamond chips set upon it. An oval box revealed a pearl necklace and after the fifth date and fifth gift she agreed to go back to his place for a glass of wine. She was a slow starter. But Josh's apartment was a shock to Leanne. It was tiny with only two rooms and smelled like her grandmother's basement after the hurricane of 1970; and it contained no real furniture.

Off to the side of the living room she could see his bedroom. The bed was on the floor and seemed to be an inflatable one. His nightstand was an upturned waste basket with a flashlight on it and a toothbrush. In the main room where she stood, his table was a cardboard box from the liquor store with "fragile" emblazoned across the sides and his armchairs consisted of two large pillows with arms; the kind that used to be popular in the 1980s. How strange, Leanne thought. She had expected his apartment to be tastefully decorated and much larger. After all, he seemed to be a man of means, able to present her with gifts each time they met. As she accepted a yellow plastic bathroom tumbler of wine and lowered herself onto the pillows set on the floor, she wondered, did he spend his entire paychecks on gifts for her? "He must really love me," she thought, as she carefully set her beaker down on a coaster that used to be a brown envelope that still showed an address on it.

At 2 a.m., when the police knocked on Josh's door with a heavy boot, and confiscated a large suitcase full of stolen jewelry, silverware and bric-a-brac, Leanne's guilty feeling about Josh spending all of his money on her quickly subsided. Not only was Josh arrested, but Leanne was also invited along to a holding cell by the arresting officers because she was wearing three stolen items. Luckily Josh came clean with the cops and absolved her of any wrongdoing. She was free to go. As she walked home with more than a hangover clouding her thoughts, she considered how her life could have changed in just a few hours.

The next day, she took "I like surprises" off her online profile, and then looked for another date.

Kenny's profile showed an attractive, slender man with eyeglasses and thick black curly hair. He described himself as liking to laugh a lot and having a great sense of humor. Leanne thought he might be the one to marry. He and Leanne dated a couple of times and his sense of humor was such that he laughed all of the time, and Leanne laughed along with him. They had so much fun. It was while at dinner on their third date that Leanne received the phone call that her Aunt Pearl had died. Leanne was heartbroken, but Kenny tried to cheer her up. "Never mind," he laughed, "I've got an aunt you can borrow if you need one!" Leanne was shocked at his flippant remark. "Ha!" chuckled Kenny. "Aunt Pearl is at the Pearly Gates now!" By the time he started singing, "My old Aunt Pearl, she liked to hurl…" Leanne was out the door.

The next day, she took "Sense of Humor" off her online profile, and then looked for another date.

By now, she was a woman who was so much wiser and only a little jaded. She reviewed Tim's profile. He looked promising. Leanne thought he might be the one to marry…

Comment

For some strange, inexplicable reason, people seem to think if you meet someone using an online dating service, your date will have already been thoroughly screened by an online fairy godmother that looks after everyone's best interests. Paying a service to get a date doesn't necessarily mean you are safe from people who are colloquially known as "crazy folk." You may still find yourself on a date with Ian the Inmate, for example, who put some cash away under a Joshua tree in the desert right after he robbed the bank. A picture may be worth a thousand words, because online it's all down to that cute smile.

When searching for a date online, take the profile information with a big, fat grain of salt, and form your own opinions. Meet in a public place where there are other people. If someone is attractive and really friendly, but somehow they seem a little creepy, go with the creepy instinct and walk away. If someone is more go-ghetto than go-getter, you'd better let her go. When your new friend chats with or meets everyone who shows interest in their online profile, it could be a prelude to cheating. It might be useful to study the faces of some famous felons before you go out on a date, so that you can familiarize yourself with criminal features, or facial expressions to avoid.

Online Dating
Handling Deceptive Daters: Where can I buy a pocket-sized lie detector?

When using the Internet to find a mate, is it O.K. to lie just a little? Or even a lot? Is everyone lying to make themselves look better than they really are, to get the edge in a competitive market? If your profile is not better than the next person's, the next person will get all the attention. So what can you do? You can lie, but you have to face the consequences. So how can you tell if someone is lying online? Easy. If they close their eyes or turn their head away when they hit "Save to Profile," they are most likely lying. They feel so guilty that they can't even look the computer screen in the eye. The tricky part is catching them at it, because at that point, you don't know them yet.

The Tale of Ewan

Ewan joined an online dating service and posted some very flattering photographs, a profile that described his college education, the usual blurb about his great sense of humor, and the kind of girl he preferred. He received many "hits," but didn't find beauty in any of the girls that were interested in him, until Kimberly gave him an online smile and he reviewed her profile.

He was drawn to the petite, slender girl with long, dark hair and big eyes who was looking for someone to fit her profile perfectly, and he asked her out online. He suggested a walk in the park might be a good way to get to know someone—no pressure, fresh air, people walking around them—a carefree atmosphere.

Kimberly was instantly attracted to his well-presented profile and he seemed like a good match for her. He was educated, had a serious and a humorous side, and they seemed to have many things in common. She accepted his invitation for a walk in the park and was excited about meeting this tall, blond man with surfer-type good looks.

They decided to meet under the black horse statue at the entrance to Roundhay Park the next Sunday afternoon. They each knew what the other looked like, so it wasn't as if it were a blind date. They both arrived on time and the park was very crowded, especially the area under the black horse because the ice cream cart was stationed there, and so was Hotdog Harry with his cart. Ewan and Kimberly searched and searched but couldn't find each other. Kimberly walked around the entranceway looking for Ewan, dodging tourists, smiling at blond men who seemed to look straight through her, but found no Ewan.

Ewan waited for a while under the statue of the horse, then walked around to the other side and waited there for a while. There were many petite girls with long dark hair and he smiled at each one, but either they stuck their noses in the air and walked by, or their companions gave him threatening looks and he had to hurry along. He was more disappointed than angry as he walked back to the black horse statue one final time. It was now 45 minutes later, but he decided to walk into the park anyway, find a bench and call her. It was a hot, sunny day and as he sat on the bench he reached into his pocket for his phone to call Kim, but realized he had left it in his car. "Who cares?" he muttered to himself, "I've lost interest in her anyway," and he watched the children playing until he gradually fell asleep.

The sun was halfway down and the bench shook slightly as a heavy, red-headed lady came and sat down next to him, waking him up. As he stretched, she smiled at him. "Hot day," she said, wiping the sweat from her forehead. Ewan agreed with her and he could tell she was happy to find someone agreeable to talk to. "I've been walking through the park for two hours," she explained, "I'm exhausted." Ewan smiled and she smiled back at this funny little man, who had a graying patch of hair and a birthmark in the shape of swan in the middle of his forehead. The sweating lady stuck out her hand in polite greeting. "I'm Kimberly," she said, introducing herself.

Ewan was somehow charmed by her. He smiled, stood up and shook her clammy hand. "I'm Ewan," he said. "Glad to meet you. Would you like to get some ice cream?"

"I'd love to," she responded. "You know, you don't look a bit like your online picture. So whose photo DID you use?"

"My brother-in-law's," he replied. "How about you?"

"An actress from the TV Guide," she responded, slipping her arm into his as they walked off into the sunset.

Comment

Taking your mother's advice about not lying is the best advice, because lying to get a date doesn't usually get you "happy ever after." You would be lucky to make it to date number two. But if both parties are lying, that's like two wrongs making a right. Online dating is the only time that can work, but be careful, deception can also have a double-edged ending.

Online Dating
Sneaky Behavior: What's that thing in your pocket?

Talking to a stranger face to face without alcohol or a good buddy at your side can be intimidating. Meeting people online eliminates this nerve-racking step to getting to know someone. If you are rejected, you just move on to the next person, or you go away, make some coffee, do some laundry and try your luck later on. The best part is that there's no one there to laugh at you or make you feel like a failure, except maybe your dog, Ruffy, but you wouldn't really consider him a judgmental creature. It's so easy for people who already have people, to meet people online. Thanks to the Internet, they can have more people to flirt with and make arrangements to meet, while their spouse sits in the other room eating chips and innocently watching CSI reruns on the TV.

The Tale of Lauren

When Lauren responded to a good looking, interesting-sounding man in an online ad, she and Justin met and immediately hit it off. After they had been dating for around three months, Lauren felt comfortable with him. Their relationship was friendly, with a dousing of romantic moments, peppered with many hours together at her house. One balmy Saturday afternoon in late August, Justin was at her home and as they sat together on the couch, Justin moved in for a hot and heavy kiss. Right before lip-impact, Lauren glanced down and noticed he was wearing what looked like a gold wedding band. At exactly the same moment, Justin also looked down and suddenly noticed that he was wearing a wedding band, and it was hard to tell who was more surprised.

Justin continued moving in for that passionate kiss, and by kissing her at something of an angle he was able to manipulate her head in the opposite direction to his ring-wearing finger, and he simultaneously tucked his hand under his elbow. It felt to Lauren like there was some non-erotic squirming going on during that kiss. It was as though he was surreptitiously trying to remove a wedding ring and stuff it into his jacket pocket, but that couldn't be the case. Justin wasn't married. He was single, like she was. He had told her so.

While the alleged ring hovered for a nanosecond in limbo between Justin's wedding finger and the safe haven of his pocket, a female index finger shot out to capture it. The ring-toss was completed more expertly than it could have been at any funfair, as a slender, manicured index finger hooped the prize.

"Aha!" cried Lauren, brandishing the ring on her finger as if she were flipping him a first-fingered bird. "What's THIS?" They both knew full well what it was.

"I don't know," he responded feebly. "Maybe it's a lemon lifesaver. I just found it between the couch cushions."

Confrontational squirming followed, and then Justin admitted to being happily married with several children who, Lauren found out, were the likeness of him. He also admitted to having two cell phones, one which he used to call his wife and family and one he kept locked up in the glove box of his car, for his philandering. When Lauren asked him why he did it, he replied, "Just for the sex. I like the variety." And then, as a back-handed compliment he added, "but I like you the best out of all the other girls." He didn't want to burn his bridges because after all, it was still early and a chance remained of him getting lucky with her that afternoon. A back-handed compliment is usually asking for a back-hander and Lauren gave him a back-handed slap, right across his right cheek, leaving an indentation of the wedding ring, just to remind him of his forgotten vows.

Comment

It seems this is more common with online folk than people would care to believe. Sinful spouses have found a way to meet members of the opposite sex while relaxing cozily at home with their families. They can secretly cyber-meet, develop a friendship, flirt, and when they find the time to meet, because they already "know" each other, they feel comfortable enough to move right into sex. So the foreplay is done right there in the marital home with a virtual stranger.

How can you tell if someone is cheating on you before you even start a relationship with them? If your new partner is adamant you don't see their home, be cautious. Ask a lot of questions to find out as much as you can about them. If you don't know how to extract information from someone, get some tips by watching how the detectives wheedle information from suspects on TV. Be good cop, bad cop, all by yourself.

Online Dating

Looking for a Date: "Needs to be rich, weak and vulnerable"

nline dating is like a blind date but without the guiding hand of the friend who would normally make the introduction. It's kind of like going to the middle of downtown, standing outside a Starbucks and counting 10 members of the opposite sex as they walk out. The 10th is yours, no questions asked. It's that random. Well, it's more of a calculated random because factoring in the posted photograph, description, likes and dislikes, makes it less of a handicap. But remember, not many people are going to list "amateur prison tattoos" in the "Biggest Regrets" column.

The Tale of Meg

Steve was excited about meeting Meg, whose photograph showed a curvy 26 year old woman with short, brown hair.

Her interests included movies, jewelry making and Steve's passion, coin collecting. They skipped the pre-date phone call because they both agreed by email that they had so much in common it would be a waste of time chatting over the phone. They instead decided to meet that night in a trendy bar by the railway station. When Steve saw Meg, he discovered that her picture didn't do her justice. She was so much more beautiful and had a soft, sexy voice that she said was caused by smoking when she was twelve. Their first date went so well, it continued on into the night and Meg found herself staying over at Steve's apartment following drinks and dinner. Then more drinks.

The next morning, Meg awoke very early and tiptoed out of bed, leaving Steve sleeping with a rosy glow of post-sex contentment on his face. She gently bent down and gave him an affectionate kiss goodbye on the cheek. Walking over to his jeans that were hung neatly on the chair, she put her hand into the pockets and removed all of his coins to add to her coin collection. There were also bills in there—dollar bills, twenties and tens and she took all of them to add to her bills collection. Looking inside a box on the dresser she found three watches and two gold chains. These would be perfect to add to her jewelry collection! It was such a coincidence he collected the same things that she did!

Before she left, she browsed his movie library and realized that he had many titles she liked but didn't yet own. Stuffing the DVD's that she wanted into her oversized handbag, she thought how lucky it was that they had met. They did have a lot in common and they got along really well. As she tiptoed out of his house, she thought it amazing that their tastes were so alike and she was thrilled at how much he was able to "offer" her. She was so glad they had met.

Comment

Steve was pretty much dating a complete stranger. Most people have extended multiple telephone conversations with a prospective online mate before they meet. One can often get a feel for someone during a conversation, either because of something they say, or just by their tone. If someone says, "I think small animals are cute," that would be a harmless statement, but if it's said in a hostile manner through clenched teeth, you may be led to believe that this person may prefer to cook and eat small animals, rather than pet them. So deciphering their tone is key.

Most importantly, don't do all of the talking yourself. Listening to a prospective partner gives you knowledge about them. You learn by listening, not by talking. Once they get comfortable talking about themselves, they may inadvertently give you some insight into their lives. For example, a man might say, "I can't meet you that far away because of my court-ordered ankle bracelet," or "Don't worry, I won't hurt you if we go out." Either one of those comments would be beneficial in helping you make the To Date or Not To Date decision.

Alternatively, it might be intimidating to a man if a woman were to say, "Let's have dinner at the place next door to the wedding ring store so that we can browse there afterward." Or, "I love big families. I want three kids with you, and then with the five I already have, we'll be one big happy family!"

Your first meeting has to be water-tight safe, and for that reason, afternoon dates in public places are often the norm, because people only get crazy at night especially if there's a full moon. It makes strangers more dangerous, or so the stories go. But needless to say, daytime dating is often safer as alcohol is not generally involved to the degree it is at night, and more people tend to be around in the daylight hours. It also eliminates the possibility of being dragged into the shadows and being beaten, raped or robbed. A short date is also recommended, just in case your soon-to-be love-interest smells like a rainy day at the bat enclosure. You get the picture—play it safe.

Online Dating
Putting Forward a Bad Impression:
How do you spell "hansum?"

It's unfortunate, but some people just don't look good on paper. You could be Mr. or Ms. Perfect Catch, but you don't translate well in an online description. You may not be good with words. If correctly written, your profile might read:

"Man, looking for single lady; ready for a committed relationship; likes walks on the beach; mystery movies; animals; is pleasant to be around."

But instead it might read:

"Committed Man, looking for single laddie; relationship; likes works on the beach. Likes misery moovies; anymules; is pleasant to be, and round."

Someone reading this profile might picture a man writing from a lunatic asylum; who is searching for a young lad. He works on the beach. He likes depressing movies and donkeys. He is pleasant, but overweight.

Your profile is something you need to spend quite a bit of time on. Get help or plagiarize. Steal other people's profiles and change them to suit your own. Use spell check or a dictionary. Have a friend read your profile out loud to you to see if it makes sense and to get another opinion on your phrasing and grammar. Your profile could make or break your opportunity for a new relationship.

The Tale of Aidan

Aidan was a gifted man at work. He was a master saucier and created wonderful tasty sauces and gravies at a hotel restaurant downtown. His spelling and grammar were quite horrendous, but it didn't matter too much at his job, because there was little writing to be done and his reading ability was standard. When he set about to draft an online profile, he was too ashamed to ask anyone for help. After he had typed it out, he was quite happy with the result. He noticed that even the computer seemed to be impressed, as it had underlined many of the best words in red.

After drafting and posting his profile online, many weeks went by and not one response was received. Aidan was misserabal, wurryed and wandered why no one had replyed to him. He changed his photograph several times, but that didn't make any difference at all. When he finally received an e-mail, it was from a woman named Ruby@LoversTiff.com and she wrote that she sympathized with his problem and said she could help him with it. Ruby recommended he look at her website and then call her.

As far as he knew, Aidan didn't have a problem, except that he was lonely. He assumed she must support a marriage guidance website, because her email address was called Lover's Tiff and as far as he knew, a lover's tiff was a lover's quarrel. Maybe she assumed he had a fight with a lover and that's why he was looking for an online mate. Perhaps she had a dating website and wanted to sell him a membership. He had nothing to lose by looking, because after all, her response was the only one in his inbox.

It was the strangest thing. Ruby's website was about male sexual problems and had nothing to do with a lover's tiff. He discovered that the website was meant to be read as Lover Stiff, not Lover's Tiff. This Ruby must be some kind of pervert, he decided. Why else would she try to sell him male enhancement products? There was nothing wrong with his equipment and he decided she must be one of those spammers.

As the weeks went by, Aidan received no other interest in his online ad and he resigned himself to the fact that he would be spending the rest of his life alone. He went on to create some wonderful sauces that withstood the trends of all times, some of which he won prizes for in international contests, and he was even interviewed for *Saucie Saucy* magazine in France.

He never did remove his profile from the website. It rested comfortably there like an undeliverable piece of mail in the Dead Letter Office. It read, "Hansum, Impotent chef at top restaurant with prestigious job. Loking for woman to settel down with." The loves of his life never came, but many advertisements for male enhancement products did, all because of the missing letter "R" in the word "Important."

Comment

When you post something online, there is a possibility of at least several hundred people, possibly thousands, seeing it. So dress it up, as you would dress yourself up for a wedding. Make yourself look good for the photos; present your profile cleanly; be clear in what you say and maybe have a friend help you with it, as you would your bowtie. And, just a thought, if you feel the need to refer to yourself as "Important," make sure you remember the fifth letter is an "R." That way, you won't mislead people into thinking you are in need of male enhancement products. Once you are all done and cleaned up, one day for sure you'll end up being the main event in the wedding party.

Life Outside of Your Home
Preparing for the big step beyond your stoop

Being newly-released by your ex can stop you in your quest for love. Your eyes are red and swollen like those Chinese goldfish you see on U-Tube, and you really don't want the hot guy at the coffee shop seeing you looking all emotionally bruised and mutated. So you stay in and behave like a bear during winter. You hibernate, over-eat and live off your fat. But unlike the bear, after hibernation you don't want to leave your house in case someone sees how bad you look.

So you put yourself on pause until you are healed. But we are hard-wired to resume the chase and it's often just of matter of when and with whom. Although our hearts, along with our hurt feelings and anger may say, "Never again!" we need to clean ourselves up, look presentable and get out there, over the threshold of our stoop and out from the cave.

The Tale of Janet

Janet had gone the breakup-recovery route. She had over-cried, over-eaten and over-hibernated. Her free time had been spent at home alone watching TV, surfing the 'net and baking cakes as she avoided the evenings and weekends in the world just beyond her stoop. It was time to leave the cocoon of her home, to disentangle herself from comfy over-sized clothes, and time to put on a little too much make up, but she just didn't want to leave her house to socialize. There were men out there and some of them were waiting for her, but she was unprepared for life outside of her stoop. She was fashion un-savvy, street un-smart and a born-again dating virgin. And she didn't care how she looked.

Contacting her friends, getting all dressed up and then driving somewhere to meet them and socialize sounded like too much work. She noticed that a hot guy lived next door to her and she watched him through the blinds from her living room window from time to time. But it wasn't enough to entice her out. Her self-esteem had hit the ground and was scurrying around the baseboards like a foraging mouse. She knew she had to get out of the house and reclaim her life, but it was all too much effort.

One morning while she was getting ready for work she heard the noise of the garbage truck clanging and banging its cumbersome load into her street, and then she remembered she had forgotten to bring hers out. Wiping a crust of sleep from her eye she grabbed her garbage can from the garage and ran out with it. Just in time. How friendly the garbage men were! They smiled and nodded as she handed them the garbage can and they kept turning around to look at her. One of them offered to carry her can back to the garage for her. He walked in front of her, but backwards, so that he didn't have his back to her. He was so polite and Janet had read that some cultures walk backwards so as not to show the other person their back. It was a sign of respect. She was beginning to think that it was worth making the effort to leave the house if men in the outside world were so friendly and polite.

Before she closed her door she saw her hot neighbor in his garden and he smiled at her and gave her a sexy leer as she went back into the house. Wow! All of these attentive men had been waiting for her just outside her stoop and she had never noticed how easy it was to attract them! She never had that kind of success before. Her self-esteem rose up, lingered around her erogenous zones and put a smile on her despondency as she closed the door.

Her day had been brightened up and she did a twirl as she switched on the radio on her way to the coffee maker. As she poured hot coffee into her stainless steel thermos, she caught sight of herself reflected in the metal. Her image looked back at her, distorting her face as if she were looking into a funfair mirror, but what was that bright pink blob on her head? She knew she wasn't wearing a hat. Fixed to the spot she backtracked to her morning routine. Where was the shower in her morning routine? Before or after garbage pickup? And what color was her shower cap at the moment? Pink? No! Pink was last month's color. So what was on her head? She sat down and thought about it as she took a bite of cold toast. Noticing her pale blue push-up bra was worn and grayed around the edges, she pulled her buttonless robe closely around her body. One day she would find the belt for it, or even sew on one of the buttons. And those long granny panties that had too many rounds with the clothes dryer needed to be replaced as they hung unevenly down beyond her thighs.

But wait a minute—her robe never stayed closed and she had just been wearing it outside,

dragging out the garbage can with an audience of men around. She had even bent down to pick up the lid when it fell off! Her shapeless robe had been open for the entire world to see, and pretty much everything she had was exposed for inspection. Her depression had led to laziness and because of that, the whole street had been invited to a grubby lingerie party just beyond her stoop. Why didn't one of the men tell her, or indicate with a shake of his head that she was exposing herself? Because they were enjoying the show. And the man walking backwards wasn't showing respect, he was just staring at her exposed body.

She shook her head in disbelief and a large pink foam hair curler plopped onto her bedroom slipper. So that's what was pink on top of her head. She felt numb as she looked at the bunny face on the slipper on her left foot, and it didn't surprise her that the other slipper was missing a head. When did that happen? Was her life passing her by as she hibernated?

It was time to get a grip and find the Janet that had been lost for too long. It was time to dress her up nicely and push her out the door and well over the stoop. But not before she made herself presentable. Now was the time to begin a thorough clothes cleansing.

Comment

Don't wait until your clothes are falling off you in rags to remind you that life goes on around you without quitting. Hibernating is good for bears but bad for people. Sometimes depression can cause you to hibernate a bit too long but trust in your nose to tell you how long is too long. The human body is amazing in its simplicity. Our noses are situated in the most efficient location on our bodies—inches away from our underarms to tell us when we need to bathe, and over our mouths so we can smell food before we eat it, to either kick-start our salivary glands or tell us that it's expired. If you are avoiding mirrors because your face is puffy, listen to your nose telling you that it's time to clean up your act.

William Shakespeare's quote about the world being a stage and everyone an actor comes to mind for this anecdote. Any time you are outside your home, you are on the stage of life—pimpled, buttonless, holes in your clothes and greens in your teeth for everyone to see, and if you are undressed, they will see that too and They Will Stare. If you want your audience to be likeable and not lecherous, you have to dress and behave accordingly, with a little leeway permitted in a dark bar with drunken patrons.

Men may not care too much if a woman is wearing curlers as long as her lingerie is showing, but Miss Manners would say that you should feel embarrassed. Likewise, a guy might not care if the neighbors see him in his grimy tightie-whities, but women will shudder, and not in a nice way. So take pride in how you look, even if you are depressed because there is always someone, somewhere judging you. When you leave the house and take that step over your stoop into the outside world—dress up for it!

Entertaining Yourself
There are better places to visit than the local asylum

*T*here's nothing more exciting than an adventure. Perhaps you see yourself trekking through the desert on a camel or sailing the ocean on a dugout canoe that you built yourself. Maybe Mount Everest is your challenge or you would love to fly an airplane. Jason was a man with adventure in his heart and too much time on his hands. There was no holding him back from taking that Greyhound bus to nowhere.

The Tale of Jason

Most weekends, Jason felt lethargic throughout his body, as though he were running in a dream and going nowhere. He was just plain bored. Since Monica left him for Jimmy, the randy Scotsman who worked at McSudsy & McLean's Laundromat, he found he had too much free time on his hands. He decided to rebuild his house exactly as he wanted it, and he spent most of his free time on that construction project. He bought an old car and took it apart and worked on it when he was tired of working on the house. Even though both the house and the car were ongoing projects, he still seemed to have too much free time and an overabundance of energy. TV and computer games filled his evenings, but he was restless. He needed some adventures.

Waking up at 5 a.m. one Saturday morning, he threw some clothes and necessities into a duffel bag and took a taxi to the bus station. He would have taken his car, but it was still in pieces in his backyard. He was on his way to have a weekend adventure.

To make this trip exciting, the weekend's destination was to be unknown to him until he reached the bus station. He decided ahead of time to take any bus leaving from Gate 3, because this trip was to be all about risk-taking and the unfamiliar. He could have picked any gate number, but three was his lucky number and also his birthday date. As the taxi pulled into the bus station, a bus was already waiting to leave from Gate 3 and Jason hurriedly paid the taxi driver and ran to catch it. Just as he reached the back of the bus, a huge cloud of evil-smelling exhaust fumes blew up into his face and ballooned around him, creating a temporary warm toxic headache as the bus roared out of the station. As Jason looked remorsefully at his missed bus—no—his lucky bus, he saw a teenager in the back seat smile, then stick his tongue out at him.

He wandered dejectedly into the waiting room to find out the time of the next bus from Gate 3, and where it would be going; and he wondered sadly at what kind of adventure he had missed by not taking the bus that had just left. Perhaps that trip would have turned his life around. It could have been the weekend to remember, but now it was ruined. Perhaps it was a bus to a city with beautifully designed architecture; maybe the destination was a cute little village with a scenic river running through it. He would never know. He felt very depressed as he looked at the departure board. But as fate would have it, Jason was lucky that day, because the bus he had just missed was the visitor's bus to the penitentiary, and that wasn't quite the adventure he was hoping for. And most likely, not the kind of people he would want to spend time with, but then again, they could probably teach him a thing or two. The next bus from Gate 3 was headed to St. Louis, and humming a medley of songs about St. Louis, he bought himself a ticket.

It was an enjoyable weekend and he made a friend on the bus named Alan who said he was a retired dentist, but once Jason caught a glimpse of two rows of misshapen, grey pointy teeth, he thought the man was probably lying. But they chatted together through the night and said goodbye as buddies in St. Louis. Jason enjoyed his trip and thought he would take another mystery trip. He opened the dictionary at random and picked out a word. Mascot. Great. He would go to Mascot, wherever that was.

Looking at his map of the United States, he discovered there was a Mascot in Tennessee and he decided that would be as good a place as any to visit. He decided to take his hot rod, as it had now been assembled into one functioning piece and he headed due west for the Mascot Motor Motel. The night before he left, he researched the area and looked for tourist attractions on the way, in case there wasn't much to do in Mascot.

He reserved a room in a popular area, because those areas are generally the furthest away from pimps, whores and murderers who live on the Bad Side of Town. But Mascot didn't have a bad side of town. It was pleasant and the country music he listened to on his state of the art car radio was strangely uplifting.

From that weekend on, every two months he visited a new place, choosing the destination name randomly from the dictionary. His traveling took him to Sandwich, Massachusetts, Likely, California, Yellowjacket, Idaho and Intercourse, Pennsylvania. He tried to make it to Nothing, Arizona, but everyone had moved away and the town was all closed up. His relationship with Monica was soon forgotten as he traveled to all places wordy and worldly.

Comment

Jason chose some interesting diversions to pass away the time and had many adventures on his own. Traveling alone as he did may not appeal to most people, but how often do we miss opportunities because we are waiting for someone to do them with us? If you still feel like half of a partnership after a breakup, it might feel strange to engage in activities without your ex. They were your guide when you drove; the expert critic when you picked out movies together; and the flavor-chooser of your ice cream sundae and toppings. "No, don't get sprinkles again, get nuts this time!" Now you are facing the task of creating your own entertainment and deciding all by yourself what kind of ice cream to have. You are going to have fun alone. This is mandatory.

This might be the time that people are firing the "Get" sentences at you. "Get a grip! Get on with your life! Get out of the house! Get over him/her!" Easily said and even harder to do if you don't have family and friends on tap to call and say and, "Hey, how would you like to…?" So you are tempted to stay at home and have no more fun in your life. Why are you punishing yourself? Haven't you punished yourself enough during this breakup? Get out! Get moving!

Go and see that movie no one else wants to see. Take a walk in the rain alone, you don't always need a companion. Have little adventures along the way. Make yourself a stronger person by being independent. You don't need old what's-their-name to make decisions for you. Do you really think your ex has turned into a shut-in? Not likely.

So what is fun to do alone? Take each letter of the alphabet and think of an interest that begins with that letter, then try it. Sometimes an activity that you tried and didn't enjoy can lead you to another one that you like better. Often, activities can be done in a group setting or with other people. You don't need friends for this, you can make some along the way. Here are some ideas:

Astronomy; bowling; collectibles; day trips away somewhere; eating out alone; fondue making; gardening, or get some plants for your home; hiking; internet games; jam making; karate; line dancing; mountain climbing or just reading about it; NASCAR or needlework; origami; photography; quarter horse racing; roller blading; Spanish lessons; train riding; understudy at a play; volunteering (information can be found at your library or online); writing short stories or songs; xylophone playing or learning a musical instrument; yoga; zumba. You don't have to be good at anything; you just have to be interested.

If you decide to follow Jason's example, however, be careful when traveling alone and don't do what Jason's friend, Isaac, did. He went to the bus station to have a mystery trip like Jason's, but didn't want to know where he was going until he looked at the ticket. Did he accidentally take that bus to the penitentiary? Nope. He had a more harebrained idea. He gave $100 to a man in the waiting room and told him, "Get me a round trip bus ticket to anywhere. I want to be surprised when I arrive. You can keep the change."

The police were quick to arrest Isaac for buying drugs from a known dealer and his story just didn't wash with them. They had heard every excuse a criminal could make, but they did find Isaac's story about giving money to a stranger to buy a bus ticket to an unknown destination an original one. Isaac's mystery trip turned out to be to a destination closer to home than he intended, and a very safe place indeed. One could even say, secure. Doing things alone is good, but safety is important and common sense is priceless. As is bail, sometimes.

Single and Two Decades Older
Moving up a generation without using the stairs

Have you ever seen those science fiction programs where people are transported into the future and everything is shiny and silver, and electronics rule the world? Sometimes life is like that. You get older. Your hair turns silver and you find yourself surrounded by electronics that you don't understand. If you are still in a relationship, these things are often ignored, but if you become single again, it's all about dying the hair to hide the silver and taking computer classes.

For you, the time has passed where you can hang out with college friends in bars to meet hot prospects to hook up with, and you might find that going dancing is just too hard on the knees. Your testosterone level has diminished, so your sex drive may be on hiatus and not available to push you out the door to seek missionary-position sex. Even a calm date with someone at the movies is too much of an effort. You worry that the shrill creak of your joints will further damage your hearing.

When Billy and Maria went their separate ways after being married to each other all of their adult lives, they found the single life much different than it had been when they were young and courting.

The Tale of Billy

Billy's friends felt sorry for him after his breakup, and they felt it their responsibility to introduce him to eligible women. Marcia was the first. She was slightly younger than he was, but moved slowly, like a cricket with chafed thighs after too much singing, and she made him nervous because she was always standing behind him, instead of next to him. Tired of looking over his shoulder all the time, he gave up on her and moved on to Tessa. Tessa was a stern, fussy woman who smoothed down his wild eyebrows with her spit and wiped his mouth with a napkin dipped in her water glass while they were out to dinner. This type of nurturing made him feel like an elderly offspring with one foot in the halfwit juncture, and anyway, the spit made his eyebrows itch. So it was goodbye Tessa.

Valerie was the third lady in the line of blind dates, and was a living, breathing, walking doting grandmother. Each date she had with Billy was a refresher course for him on her grandchildren - Annabelle, Julie and little Thammy with the lisp. A few more blind dates followed and none of them were memorable, so Billy was relieved when his friends gave up on him and stopped introducing him to the single women they knew. Oddly enough, he didn't need an adjustment period to being alone, he just resumed his old habits from his days of being single, and everything settled down tidily. Just like wood chips mulching a garden, a healthy balance was restored and the old pre-marriage habit of having drinks in bars with friends was re-established.

But Billy had a secret weapon—he was a salesman and a pretty damn good one too. Some things are not lost with age; many talents become more polished and shiny with experience, and, as everyone knows, women are attracted to all things polished and shiny, as are magpies. His plan was simple and consisted of the first piece of sales advice he had ever been given in his teenage years, "Keep asking for the order until you get a yes." When Billy began to apply it to dating, by the law of averages it began to work. He asked out every woman he liked, and when they began saying no, he politely moved on to the next one. All of that cold calling in his past had made him tough when rejection poured the icy water of "No!" in his face. Trying is merely a numbers game and as long as you never stop trying, someone, somewhere will give you a "Yes!"

Billy was astounded at how many women said "yes" to him, even though the "no's" were more frequent at around 90 percent. The ones who said "yes," found him charming, persuasive and funny. Many friendships followed, perhaps because he was older and definitely because he was low-key. The ladies he took out felt that he gave them space and put few demands on them, and his conversation was light-hearted. Some were looking for a real relationship, and others just went along for the ride, for laughter or companionship. And Billy was the man to give it to them. An old sales trick had moved him into the new century.

The Tale of Maria

Maria tried lots of things that didn't work. She went to bars with women from work, but found the music too loud and drinking alcohol these days made her feel sleepy instead of sexy. Men of all ages gravitated to the younger women in the group and she realized that men who went to bars were not looking for a woman like her. She took a class in basic plumbing to meet men, and she met four of them who were happy to help her with her pipe couplings, but not her love-couplings. Friday evenings were spent at local singles' dances where the men stood at one end of the room and the women at the other end, looking furtively across at each other in the same way a witness would search for a perpetrator in a police lineup. She met some very nice people there, Annette, Janice and Hayley, but sadly, few suitable men crossed the line into their enemy territory.

Maria felt as though she had just stepped out of a time warp because everyone was talking about lines that she had never heard of: online, offline, landline, dateline. She was more familiar with feminine lines, such as hemlines, clotheslines, and waistlines. She preferred men with hairlines who were streamlined, and she particularly like framed pictures of scenes with coastlines and skylines. She remembered vividly that the first line Billy had ever given her was when he talked her into having sex with him when she was 19. Her wedding was step two of her pregnancy and the rest of her life was followed by marriage. Billy had always been her lifeline.

Soon Maria surrendered to the lines of the current century and began online dating. Her hopefulness at meeting the right someone out there began to fade as she became tired of sifting out the married men, avoiding the misfits, being polite to the boring ones and picking up the check for the cheapies. Defeated, she gave up her quest for the ideal man and decided to be happy without any strings attached. Once she had decided to stop looking so hard for a relationship, she found herself easy to be around and her life became enjoyable. She adopted a kitten from the animal shelter and named her Tumbles. It was good to have something friendly in the house, and pretty soon Maria began to smile again, and sing 70's songs to herself while she baked gingerbread men, then ate the heads off each one, broke off the arms and…well, we all carry a little pent-up anger!

It wasn't until people started smiling at her that she realized she had been smiling at them. No, it wasn't because of age-related memory loss or good tranquilizers; she was just more relaxed at being herself, which made her happy. Neighbors, grocery store cashiers, hobos, people out walking, and even a youth in the emergency room who was on a morphine IV returned her easy smile. After that, the conversation flowed. Once she started relaxing and becoming the person she felt she really was, instead of the person she thought others would like her to be, the effort of trying hard to meet someone disappeared and the desperation was all but gone. Sometimes men would chat to her about their spouses and the conversation was friendly. Other times men asked her out because she was relaxing to be around and life flowed over her instead of forcing a way in. Maria began meeting men she wanted to date and she was able to choose her own speed.

Comment

So, you lost your love after decades of being together. You feel cheated because you are back where you started and it all looks too familiar. But déjà vu always looks familiar, and even though it's French and you've never been to France, you know you've been here before, but a long, long time ago. People of all ages face challenges when newly-single. Some people have moved along a generation or two and feel like they are infringing on young people's territory when they try to meet people. This is not so, because each generation has its own territory. You just have to find out where the borders begin and end. You may have been out of style for several decades, but just like those pointy-toed black and white shoes of your youth, everything comes back into fashion, including you, and history repeats itself.

Hardships grow like baby boll weevils on a cotton flower and some people leave relationships that were infested with abuse or neglect. Others become single and face low self-esteem. Many just feel tired and old. Does knowing that make it any easier? It should. You now have maturity and more patience than before, and the crazy things in life won't get to you as much. You are less impulsive and that might be the constraint that stops you from falling on your face and looking like a fool. Although, living in the wrong decade and wearing tie-dye headbands can also have the same effect, so make sure you read a current magazine before you strut out with those gigantic padded shoulders or the same big hair-style you wore on your wedding day.

Rebuilding
Getting sticky in a web of determination

One of the most traumatic memories from your childhood might have involved having your pains-takingly built sandcastle brought down by an over-enthusiastic wave, or perhaps a wild brother stabbed your Lego dinosaur right through its plastic heart with a toy sword. Maybe you built up the sandcastle again, or punched that damn annoying brother of yours in the arm, but what-ever you did, you learned that the need to rebuild is often a part of life and always will be.

Many of the creatures we share this earth with are build-ers and rebuilders. Like us, they build relationships, homes, stores of food; all the basic requirements of life. We may feel superior to these creatures, but still admire the efficiency of ants before crushing them, or the intricate design of a wasp's nest built on our front porch before we guiltily knock it down with a broom handle. But we do share some aspects of their bad luck. What we have in common is that we spend time putting things together, and then a careless creature comes along and knocks down the fruits of our labor. We could call this careless creature "Our Ex." A breakup can make our lives fall hard to the ground and we have to pick ourselves back up again. Just like a bird's nest hit by a tornado, we have a lot of rebuilding to do.

The Tale of Darius

Every morning, Darius would make his way to his car in space number 9 to drive to work. One damp September morning he noticed a large brown spider had constructed an elaborate web from an adjacent birch tree to the passenger side mirror of his car. The web was large and Darius thought it must have taken more than a day to construct. After all, he was an engineer and knew about such things.

Through the early morning fog, he stood and watched the spider efficiently finishing the trap so it could feast on a fly-steak meal later on that day. As Darius watched it working so hard, he idly wondered if it drank from the dew that laced the web. But now it was getting late and writing bad spider poetry in his head wasn't something he had time for. Climbing into his car, he turned the key and shifted it into reverse as he did every morning, then glanced at the web. As he gently put his foot on the gas, he saw the web stretch just a little bit and he slammed on the brakes. Could he be so heartless? Of course he could. Only a Tibetan monk with a vow to safeguarding any living creature would be unable to pull out. But Darius? He was a western man and knew nothing of eastern philosophies. He was a much weaker man since Keisha left, but nevertheless a man. He gunned the gas pedal and before the tires shrieked a strangled scream, he heard a tiny, almost imperceptible sound of a damp spider web slapping his windshield. The sound would haunt him for about a minute, and by the time he reached Kalischer Street, the memory was temporarily gone.

Darius arrived at work feeling somehow dejected, but he wasn't sure why. Killing a bug here and there was something that had never fazed him, so there was no reason why spider murder would be on his mind. A cup of coffee and several phone calls later, the spider was soon forgotten until the next morning. Then history repeated itself. Nothing had changed from the previous day, except of course that the web was new, and maybe a tiny bit bigger? Hands in pockets and guilt in his heart for what he was about to do again, Darius looked at the new web. How could such a small creature have built such a large intricate structure in just one night? It was symmetrically perfect. He saw that there were already some tiny struggling black flies kicking their legs around in one corner and a dry moth propped upright in another. To rebuild such an extravagant web must have taken all night. But that's what insects and other small-brained creatures do—they work to eat, and when they rest, they sleep and presumably dream about food because watching television or going shopping is out of the question.

That morning Darius was being tough. Teeth clenched and radio blasting, he backed out of his parking place, and by the time he looked through the windshield, all that was left of the web was a smear of sticky spider silk. Every night that week the spider wove a perfect new web and every morning Darius and his car tore it down, leaving the brown spider hanging by a single, glistening thread, seemingly shaking one of its tiny fists at Darius, as if it had such a limb.

But the persistence of the spider rebuilding its web caused Darius to reflect on his own life, which had been difficult since he and Keisha had divorced, and now, like the spider, he was trying to rebuild it. He missed the luxuries he had worked so hard for in the past, but at least he knew where they were. They were still inside his big, bright house that no longer belonged to him. Darius had to swallow his resentment and be strong, and rebuild his life. Thus the plight of the spider became his inspiration, as it had been to Robert the Bruce, who was once King of Scotland. "If the spider can rebuild its home and life over again, so can I," Darius told himself. He also felt very grateful that he didn't have to build a web every day, because going to work was tough enough.

Ten days and ten webs had passed, and Darius was now in the habit of parking his car further back in space number 9 when he returned from work, so that the spider couldn't use it as scaffolding for its web, forcing it to build a web between the lowest branches of the birch tree.

Over the next few months Darius became successful in his business and he was successfully rebuilding his life. He credited the spider for his inspiration. One evening, as he was leaving his car to walk to his apartment, he gave his customary Good Evening salute to Big Bertha, the spider, but instead of seeing her busily working on her web, she was curled up in a ball in the center of her sticky home. Hardworking Bertha had died sometime during the day. Darius hoped that she had passed away peacefully in her sleep and not through the exhaustion of building so many webs. Happily, after some research, Darius discovered that it only takes a spider an hour to build a web, which they usually rebuild every night, because as time goes on the stickiness weakens. Darius was learning a lot from an arachnid.

Because he had such a fondness for the creature and the lesson she had taught him, he tenderly lifted her out from her sticky dwelling and put her in a little glass dessert dish on a shelf in his home, where the stiff, brown, curly little creature could be an inspiration to him every day. When his new girlfriend, Janie moved in, she found the dusty carcass repulsive and threw her out. It was a sign of the times to come, but that's another story.

Comment

Motivation can be found all around us, you just need to be able to recognize it. If Darius was inspired by something so tiny, just think how much encouragement can be drawn from something even a little bit bigger. Many things in this world are bigger than a spider and it's likely that some of them are just as inspirational, so keep your eyes open for anything that can help encourage you as you struggle along.

A great place to read about struggles is the bible, which is full of stories of toil and torment. If you think your troubles are bad, they will seem like nothing compared with Lot's wife being turned into a pillar of salt or unlucky folk being stoned to death. While the bible is full of words like wrath, despondency and strife, it also carries words of encouragement like hope, salvation and comfort, which can easily become inspiring to many people, and help them rebuild.

Some people find that listening to inspirational CDs help them, because they like being told what to do and at a time like this, it's hard to think for yourself. Occasionally, something on television might strike a motivational note, so make sure you have a pen and paper ready when you sit down to watch talk shows, sport or reality TV. Not to mention documentaries that show how the world around us is changed by rebuilding, one little web at a time. Even cartoons can encourage us to get up and dust ourselves off— look at Wile E. Coyote and the Road Runner! There is no more perfect example of never giving up. No, it's not easy, and looking around at the people in our lives, we see successes, but rarely do we see the difficulties that people go through in order to be successful. Everyone struggles, you just can't give up.

Being inspired by something or someone is the antidote to struggling. It's a prescription for a tiny dose of motivation, which should be taken three times a day, with or without food, so that it can accumulate in the body. So keep trying to rebuild, because life is all about fresh starts and moving forward. For others, it's just about working hard every day and catching flies so that you won't starve.

Let's Propose a Toast to Breakup Recovery

A Punchbowl of Therapeutic Quotes

It's Always The Darkest Before Dawn

*I*f you haven't heard this seventeenth century phrase before, you might be inclined to believe it refers to a man looking for love, and being dark and depressed until he meets Dawn, the girl from the flower shop. It might also mean that as the night progresses, it gets darker and darker and then, just before the sun comes up, the night has reached its darkest time. Maybe this was the case back in the 1600's, but these days it gets progressively lighter before the dawn, not darker. Perhaps the sense of observation was not as keen back then, or maybe people just drank too much wine and slept through it.

When you find yourself going through a bad time, it seems like it will never end. And then, things get worse. So you struggle along, being brave, strong and devastated, and after a while you kind of get used to it and you stop crying and have less pity-me days and life goes on. Then suddenly, out of the blue, along comes Dawn to save the day, marching in with a gleam in her eye and her skirt just a little bit too short.

However, the dawn in the famous quote is spelled with a small "d" and is therefore not a real person, but signifies the time when the night ends and the day takes over. So the quote implies if you have been depressed all through the night, then by the first light of dawn, you will have reached your darkest, or saddest moment. But people recovering from a breakup can also be sad when the sun shines, so what the saying really means is when it seems like things will never be good again, something will come along and brighten up your life, whether it be Dawn, Brian, or just watching your favorite movie with your elderly Aunt Martha. So keep peeping behind the drapes in your imagination and watch out for the daylight coming to rescue you.

Every Cloud Has A Silver Lining

What does this saying mean and how does it apply to you? To maybe understand it better, imagine a store that has a sign that reads, "Today's Special—Every Suit on Sale Today has a Silver Lining." So you go inside the shop and every suit they have on sale has a beautiful silk, silver-colored lining, some with narrow silver pinstripes and some with tiny silver polka dots. The only downside is the suits are ugly. No, worse, they are hideous. But if you bought one of those suits, not only would you be saving money, but when you take off the jacket, and fold it just so, showing the silver lining, you would impress people and therefore be happy with your suit and with the rest of your life.

On the other hand, it might mean that the big black cloud that's been hanging over your head ever since Bobby broke up with you is only gloomy on the outside. It may have felt to you that all good things in life have been away for the season, selfishly tanning their cheer, and you have been left with only misery and gloom. Luckily, this is only temporary, because John Milton, who coined the "Silver Lining" phrase in 1634, realized that every cloud does have a silver lining to it, and even though he was a poet and not a meteorologist, the saying has survived the test of time and therefore must be true. So your life *will* improve. Inside the ugly black cloud of your current life is a silver lining, just like the lining inside the hideous suits, and silver, as everyone knows, is the color of happiness and cheer. Well, at least it's bright and shiny and that's encouraging. So as things slowly get better for you, nurture your dark cloud because after a while all that dark stuff will fall off like rust and you will be happy again. Maybe even rich.

There's A Light At The End Of The Tunnel

Your life is dark at the moment. It might be that you are conserving electricity because you are alone and no longer have someone to help you pay the utility bills. Or it might be because it always seems to be the middle of the night when you are at your most active, writing bad poetry, or listening to melancholy saxophone music and thinking about lost loves. But if you have been having depressing thoughts, then suddenly feel more optimistic and lighter, it's a sign of a positive change coming into your life. You will notice a visible brightness in your peripheral vision, a freeing of the spirit, and you may now be walking with your head held up high, instead of staring at your shoes that used to kick up the powdery dusts of depression. Your breathing is becoming more relaxed and you will gradually see a glimmer of radiance in the distance, just like daylight at the end of a tunnel. What you are actually seeing is a turning point, which signifies the healing of your body and soul after all of the heartache you have been through. Of course it may also look like a train is coming towards you with its headlights on. But don't be afraid. That's probably another relationship waiting to hit you smack on.

This Too Shall Pass

You are standing out in the rain during rush hour. It's windy too, and you might have foolishly chosen to wear a short jacket along with a pleated skirt today. A man also regretting his choice of clothing may be wearing a light-colored suit that has mud splashes all the way down the back of the pants. You are miserable because the bus is late. Finally, in the mistiness of the dim day and the chill of the winter evening, you see the headlights of your bus. Looking inside you see it's so crowded that people are standing, pushed against the doors. It slows down at your stop, but then it keeps right on going. There's another one following it and the little old lady behind you says, "The next bus is also full. It too shall pass by without stopping," and she's right. It does.

Your life is similar to the crowded buses that pass you by in the rain without stopping. The fog, the cold, the bad choice of clothing are all the everyday wrong decisions and disappointing events that have been in your life for much too long now. When will it end and when will all of those bad things pass away from your life? You can never be sure of when, but just like the buses, the bad things *will* pass, leaving a sunny day with fluffy clouds, azure skies and a big, fat yellow sun smiling down on you. Well, maybe only in the poetry of your life, but it's true, all the nasty stuff will go away after time and will be washed down the drain of the past, leaving you with memories of rich experiences, and you will have recovered from your breakup. So get out of the rain, go home, take a hot bath and put a little paper umbrella in the Breakup Cocktail you've been promising yourself all day long. You've been through a lot. You deserve it, and now you begin to heal.

CPSIA information can be obtained at www.ICGtesting.com
Printed in the USA
LVOW01s0813070913

351414LV00015B/580/P

9 781480 037854